ISLANDS IN THE OCEAN

A 90-DAY DEVOTIONAL

KEVIN & KIM MILLS

MILLS Creative MINDS

Thank you for
your constant
love and support!

~Kevin + Kim

CONTENTS

Introduction

Sometimes life can be hard.

Even as Christians, filled with the Holy Spirit and saved for a glorious eternity in the future, the looming clouds of today can overwhelm us at times. Discouragement, depression and disillusionment can creep into our lives, skewing our perspective on our struggles as they attempt to drag us down. It may surprise you to hear this, but even on the mission field we wrestle with these same issues. (We know, you thought it was all sunshine and tropical paradise, didn't you?)

One of our driving motivations in writing this journal was to encourage those around us, giving hope to our own children, the dorm kids and students who call us Uncle Kevin and Aunt Kim, our family overseas, our friends spread around the globe and our supporters and prayer warriors. Everyone has given so much to us in our lives, either directly or indirectly, and we want to take this opportunity to give something back.

The world is ever-expanding, and even though we're more connected through technology than ever before, we're still half a world away from most of you and will rarely be able to spend much quality time face-to-face this side of Heaven. Despite this, we offer you these devotionals as a means of encouragement, hope and comfort. We don't pretend to know all the answers, but we've always strived to live our lives with openness and transparency, so if we can help you navigate life by sharing some of our triumphs and failures and more than a few humbling epiphanies, we're happy to help.

Like islands in the ocean, we hope the Father will use these daily words to provide you with the peace, sanctuary, safety and stability you're seeking when your life becomes a stormy sea. May you find the rest and perspective you need to continue on your journey, soaking up the lasting hope and supernatural strength only He can provide. We pray the next 90 days will minister to you in an intimate, personal way, that His Word and Spirit will speak through these pages as we share His constant love and consistent faithfulness for us all.

It is true. Life *can* be hard.

Yet despite what we might face, we can cling to the truth that God *is* good.

Even in our storms.

(*Especially in our storms.*)

Kevin & Kim

Before he had finished praying,
Rebekah came out with her jar on her shoulder.
- Genesis 24:15

The Lord of Perfect Timing

THIS STORY SOMETIMES GETS SKIPPED OVER, BUT IF WE PAUSE TO read it slowly, it will blow our minds. In Genesis 24, we see Abraham's servant has been sent to find a wife for Isaac. He starts praying a very specific prayer, asking God for a clear sign to determine which woman will be The One. And then, *before he was even finished praying*, Rebecca arrives and begins to fulfill his humble request.

Before he had even finished praying!

We need to remember this.

We need to remind ourselves that God works beyond our timeline, outside of our time constraints. He has a prepared a perfect answer to *all* of our prayers, and they have been orchestrated far in advance. We just need to believe that He is God, and He will give us *exactly* what we need, *when* He wants us to have it.

Today you are most likely in a waiting period, waiting for an answer about something or someone. You've prayed the prayers, maybe even shed a tear or two or three thousand. You're in the waiting phase with expectant, paused breath.

Have Faith.

Have faith that God has not only heard your prayer, but He has your absolute best interest and success in mind. Choose to trust Him today, no matter how long it takes before you see the answer to your prayer. He will not, *cannot* be late. He is the God of perfect timing.

"You study the Scriptures diligently because
you think that in them you have eternal life.
These are the very Scriptures that testify about me,
yet you refuse to come to me to have life." - John 5:39-40

Surrender and Die

Jesus was not happy with the Pharisees.

To be fair, they were pretty legendary in their study of the Scriptures. They could memorize large portions of the Hebrew Bible, copying it with extreme care and attention for detail (something for which we can now all be thankful). So what was the big deal? Simply put, they took great pride in their great learning.

Today technology has made it easier than ever to dive into the Bible. We have unprecedented access to all kinds of powerful and scriptural knowledge and insight into the secret things of God. We can study His word endlessly, recite it flawlessly and have a sincere passion for worship and holiness, but if we do not have a personal relationship with Jesus Christ — an experience that has transformed us from the inside out — we're just wasting our time.

Our salvation does not come from memorization or Biblical enthusiasm or performance or passion or anything else that can be measured. It comes from *surrender.*

A *surrendered* heart, a *surrendered* life to Jesus Christ, trusting that He is the *only* way we will ever see the face of God when we get to Heaven. If you haven't made the choice to give your entire life to Jesus yet, please don't put if off any longer. Today's the day!

Lord Jesus, I confess that I am a sinner and that you are the true, resurrected Son of God. I recognize that I can't be saved without You, won't be united to God without You. I recognize and accept your sacrifice on the cross, your death and resurrection, and I ask you into my heart today. Amen!

For he wounds, but he also binds up;
he injures, but his hands also heal. - Job 5:18

Broken

THE OTHER NIGHT WE WERE ENTERTAINING SOME GUESTS AND one of them accidentally dropped a glass bowl. It clattered to the ground with amazing clarity, shattering into hundreds (if not thousands) of pieces on our tile floor. Of course we reassured them it was no big deal, that it was only glass and nothing to cry about. Upon further reflection, though, the image is striking.

We live in a broken world.

We are constantly breaking others or in the process of being broken ourselves. Broken lives, broken hearts, broken spirits... sometimes it seems as if we are never in a state of completion or wholeness. Like Humpty Dumpty, we're constantly scrambling for our many pieces in an attempt to fuse them back together again.

Brokenness is where God delights in amazing us, exceeding our limited expectations. He can take the broken pieces of our lives — the shattered fragments and razor-sharp slivers — and mend them back together again. Somehow, inexplicably and *incredibly*, He's able to make them stronger than they were *before* the break.

He makes *us* stronger than we were before.

Think about it. God has the ability and desire to take your broken spirit, broken mind, broken body and yes — *even your broken heart* — and heal it. He can not only heal it to fullness, but to the point where it is actually stronger today than it ever was yesterday. Heal *you* to the point where you will finally, honestly recognize that you're stronger today than you were yesterday.

We live in a broken world. Yet we don't have to *stay* broken. Place your life back in the Potter's hands and let Him fashion something new and beautiful out of you.

"No servant can serve two masters.
He will hate the one and Love the other, or he will be devoted
to the one and despise the other." - Luke 16:13

Owning vs. Owned

How much stuff do we need to be happy in life?

It may surprise you to know that 17 of the 38 parables of Christ were focused on our possessions. In fact, possessions were mentioned 2,172 times in scripture. If that seems like a lot, you're absolutely right. That's 3x's more than **love**, 7x's more than **prayer**, and 8x's more than **belief**. Truthfully told? **Fifteen percent of God's Word deals with our** *stuff.*

We think we own our stuff, but too often our stuff starts to own *us.* We get so excited for new things, we're blinded by their true (and hidden) costs. That new TV or computer or widget might seem like *exactly* what we need, but once we get it we spend hours buried deep in a manual, setting it up and tweaking it until it's "just right."

We're addicted to the shiny and new, but newness quickly fades. Every new thing we get our hands on in the present is just one more thing that will break in the future. The sobering part? Every single thing we're so excited about *today,* that we've sacrificed for and scrambled to get... will one day end up in the dump. **All of it.**

We think if we only had "a little more" we'd finally be alright, finally be at peace. A little more money, a few more things, more *stuff,* and then our lives would reach new levels of perfection. We are such fickle creatures, each of us filled with internal and eternal holes that we forever try to patch over with *stuff.* The truth is *more* will never be *enough.* Spiritual voids can't be filled with physical things.

Do you feel like you have a handle on your stuff? Is God challenging you today to change some of your spending habits? Saving habits? Giving habits? Is there an area He's calling you to look closer at in your life to make a change?

As soon as the priests who carried the ark reached the Jordan and their feet touched the water's edge, the water from upstream stopped flowing. It piled up in a heap a great distance away... while the water flowing down to the Sea... was completely cut off. So the people crossed over opposite Jericho. - Joshua 3:15-16

First Steps

THIS IS AN INCREDIBLE SCENE. THE ISRAELITES ARE CARRYING the Ark of the Covenant and stopped at the Jordan river. The waters were raging and from every angle it looked hopeless. Without a bridge, without a clear pathway forward, how could they get from one side to the other? Humanly speaking, it was impossible.

Yet when these priests started walking toward the Jordan and their feet first touched the river's edge, the water from upstream *stopped flowing*. It just completely stopped! So they continued in the direction God had originally called them, where He had first led them, because He had made a way through.

Sometimes God will wait for us to take that first step of faith before He's willing to part the waters in our lives. All too often we're kneeling on the sidelines, praying and waiting for Him to act or clear the way, to make it *easier* for us to move forward. Many times we wait for our circumstances to be more convenient or more comfortable.

This is even true in areas of ministry, where we might feel a specific calling to do something He wants us to. Yet so many times God is waiting on *us!* He's waiting for us to exercise our *belief* and faith by coupling it with *action*.

It's not enough for us to proclaim our faith in His power and ability to part the waters in our lives. He absolutely can. Maybe you're getting impatient or afraid as you stare at what lies dead ahead of you. But *maybe He's waiting for you* to act first, to step out in faith and risk getting a little wet.

Lord, who may dwell in your sanctuary?
He whose walk is blameless... Who does what is righteous, who speaks
the truth... Who keeps his oath,
even when it hurts. - Psalms 15:1-2,4

Even When It Hurts

WEBSTER'S DICTIONARY DEFINES INTEGRITY AS *"THE QUALITY of being honest and having strong moral principles or uprightness. The state of being whole and undivided."*

When I was growing up, I never really gave the word much thought. "Integrity" was reduced to a Christianese concept that youth leaders threw around once in a while, but it wasn't until I was an adult that I finally began to fully appreciate its importance in life.

It's easy to keep a promise when people are getting along. When everything's coming up roses we'll make all kinds of commitments, pledging our loved ones the moon and more! But what happens when the roses start to wilt and we start to see the dark side of the moon? The glaring humanity in our relationships?

When we're hurt by someone — whether intentionally or accidentally — we tend to react in kind. We adopt a "you hurt me, so I'm gonna hurt you *more*" mentality, as if we suddenly regress back to elementary school. Of course, this response makes everything worse.

What if, even when we're wounded, we chose to react with integrity? What if we did what we knew was right, *even if it hurts?* Without question, integrity can sometimes be both incredibly painful and inconvenient.

Take a moment to think about your relationships. Has someone hurt you recently? (Intentionally or not) Are there areas where you feel you've been wronged? Cheated? Regardless of your circumstances or how your *heart* is steering you, ask the Lord if there's a way you might be able to respond with greater integrity, even in the middle of the mess.

He replied, "The man they call Jesus made some mud
and put it on my eyes. He told me to go to Siloam and wash.
So I went and washed, and then I could see." - John 9:11

Here's Mud in Your Eyes

SOME DAYS YOU MAY FEEL AS IF THE GOOD LORD HIMSELF
might be going out of His way to put a glob of mud in your eyes.
Maybe you were praying and hoping for something specific for a
long, *long* time, and then when God finally shows up... He
deliberately slathers mud across your face.

It's obviously not an accident. It was clearly intentional, and it
stings and it's gooey and gross and you can't help but wonder "Why-
oh-*why* would God allow this to happen to me now? Why would He
do this to me? What is even happening here?!"

It's a good question. A fair question.

But if we will hold fast to the belief that God truly is **good** and
that He really, really, *really* loves us, then we can rest knowing that
what's going on is for our good. It is. The caked, cracking dirt on your
face? It's not cosmetic. **It's *transformational*, because it's
directly and divinely from His hands.**

Sure, it might hurt and be quite unpleasant and downright
confusing and uncomfortable, but in the end?

It will be good.

It *will*. Just trust Him.

You can trust the Potter's hands.

He is a skilled and loving Creator. Always.

*Therefore no one will be declared righteous in God's sight
by the works of the law; rather, through the law
we become conscious of our sin. - Romans 3:20*

Wanted: Jesus Christ, Law Breaker

SO MANY TIMES WE GET CAUGHT UP IN TRYING TO DO "THE right thing." We're constantly trying to *say* the right thing, *be* the right person, put on the perfect Christian face and give all the right answers. It's almost as if we're ticking off individual boxes on some kind of Holiness Checklist.

Even though we died to our sins through Christ and are now considered holy, we still believe we have to *perform*, that we have to do *something* else to earn our salvation (or at least maintain it). Maybe we feel God will be disappointed with us or we'll somehow lose rank or status if we aren't always *absolutely, 100% perfect*. We trip and stumble and enslave ourselves to the law once again instead of leaning on His grace, freely given.

It is so hard for us to wrap our heads around the concept of grace. It is undeserved, it is all-encompassing and it is a free gift. Once we grasp the magnitude and power of God's grace, freely provided to us, we will stop entangling ourselves with the idea we have to "do more." The law made us conscious of death, but Jesus is *greater* than the law. **Jesus overcame the law so we could have true life.**

We naturally want to *do*, to *become*, to *please* Him, and these instincts aren't necessarily wrong. We just have to remain focused on Him, keeping everything in perspective. We're won't lose His love if we're not perfect today, and we won't get a bigger portion of it tomorrow if we are. He's already given us everything we need. We are unconditionally loved and eagerly embraced — just as we are. Right now. *Today.* Thank you, Lord!

Everyone who loves has been born of God and knows God.
Whoever does not love does not know God,
because God is love. - 1 John 4:7-8

Whoever Loves...

THIS IS A POWERFUL VERSE, AND CUTS STRAIGHT THROUGH OUR selfishness and creative justifications. It is so easy for us to become consumed with hate and resentment because of something someone else said or did to us. We're always conveniently blind to the blurry collection of our *own* faults, yet possess a keen super-sight when it comes to identifying and scrutinizing what others do to *us*.

Unfortunately, John spells out what we're doing in plain English: whoever doesn't love others *doesn't know God*. Whoever lives in love, *lives in God*. Whoever loves God *must also love his brother*.

Sure, it sounds good on paper (or on a screen, as they case may be), but when you're in the thick of it, when you're bubbling over with bitterness and rage and resentment, loving someone you don't feel deserves it can sometimes become the hardest thing in the world.

You might have to work up to it. You may have to ask God for supernatural strength. As a human being, chances are good there are a few exceptionally unlovable people floating around in your life — people whom God has perfectly placed there *for a specific reason*.

What reason is that? It's so you might step outside of yourself for a while, stretching your own limitations and reaching the end of your ability to love. Because then, and only then, will you be in a place where you can genuinely rely on Him, depending on His love to overflow through you... to them.

Hate is easy. Love is hard.

If we want to know God, we must love others.

Let us run with perseverance
the race marked out for us, fixing our eyes on Jesus,
the author and perfecter of our faith. - Hebrews 12:1-2

Trust the Author

DO YOU EVER FEEL LIKE YOUR LIFE IS SECRETLY PART OF AN ongoing movie? As if there were an invisible camera constantly hovering around you, recording everything about you — your every move, your every conversation?

It's not too far from the truth.

Your life is unfolding day by day, just like a story on a page. Your life has been *filled* with interesting characters, gripping moments of dialogue, tension, and more than likely a few tear-jerking tragedies along the way. In fact, you might recognize yourself as being smack dab in the middle of one of those tragedies *right now*.

If that's you, then please listen closely to these words: **there is hope**. Don't lose heart. *Your story, in all its dramatic glory, is still being written!* Don't give in to the temptation of thinking you've reached **The End**. You haven't. Yes, it may be you've reached the end of *this* current chapter, but the beginning of a *new* one.

We can't force the pages to turn any faster. We wish we could reach out, grab the corner and yank it from one side to the other, from the present pain into the peace He promised for tomorrow. We can't, no matter how much we want to.

But there is one thing we *can* do: Trust Him.

Trust the Author and Perfecter of your Faith.

Life is going to contain enough plot twists to make your head spin. Don't be tempted to inject a period where God is in the process of placing a comma. He's still writing your story, and you can trust Him in the process.

The way of a fool seems right to him,
but a wise man listens to advice. - Proverbs 12:15

Downhill

WHEN I WAS AROUND TEN YEARS OLD, MY FAMILY AND I WERE skiing at Winter Park, Colorado. Truth be told, I was a pretty good skier, perhaps youthfully confident to a fault. One fateful afternoon my pride led me to a fall I'll remember forever.

After exiting the ski lift, I saw my mother (with her unmistakably bright yellow and black snowsuit) leading the way down the slope. I immediately followed, impressed by her newfound speed and skills. She was fast, but I was up to the challenge and quickly bolted after her, faintly hearing my father calling from behind us to slow down.

I soon realized I had made a serious mistake when I watched her turn onto a black diamond trail and disappear from view. My mother had always been more of a safe, green circle kind of gal... the easy stuff. A crazy-steep black diamond? My mother would *never* have attempted such a thing. Ever.

Nope. I'd been following a complete stranger, and I was in trouble.

Within seconds I wiped out on the trail, falling end over end until I came to rest in a snowdrift at the outermost edge. The snow around me was at least four feet deep, and I found myself packed in tight, flat on my back, staring up at the sky.

I was frozen in place and terrified, and I screamed for help. Nobody heard me. Nobody came. My mind started racing. *Had anyone seen me wipe out? Did anyone even know I was there?* That was when I knew I was destined to die there that very night, trapped and frozen solid and utterly alone.

So imagine my relief when my father's face appeared through the narrow opening above me. He wasn't happy, but I was ecstatic to see *him*. The rest of my family were pretty upset that we then had to hike cross-country through the woods to get to a safer trail, but I was just thrilled to be *alive*.

It is so easy, so natural for us to trust in our own conclusions, ignoring the protests from friends, family and even a Heavenly Father as we careen downhill. If we'll only take the time to *slow down* and *listen* to those who love us most, we can save ourselves more than a few downfalls and detours in life.

The heart is deceitful above all things and beyond cure.
Who can understand it? - Jeremiah 17:9

Sincerely Deceitful

THE WORLD LIKES TO PLACE A LOT OF EMPHASIS ON SINCERE emotions. People are quick to justify their actions or life decisions based on the sincerity of how they *feel*, even to the point of insisting that their feelings — *all feelings* — are both natural and God-given.

But is this true?

Well, it *is* true that emotions — including a large number of desires — *are* completely natural. We all have them, in various shapes and strengths. And yes, while we feel them intensely and with utmost sincerity, does this mean our *every* desire is from God Himself?

Think about it. Compulsive thieves *truly* and *sincerely* desire to steal what is not theirs. Serial killers are *genuinely* compelled to take the lives of those around them. The adulterer has a *genuine, completely natural* and, yes, *God-designed desire* to love and to be loved by someone else.

These are just a few examples, but you can see where this line of thinking takes us. Our desires and what we decide to *do* with them are two distinctly different things. Clearly, just because somebody feels a desire — regardless of how *genuine* or *sincere* or *intense* it is — does <u>not</u> mean it is by default "God-given." **However sincere a feeling is doesn't mean it is automatically holy or good.**

We can't do whatever we feel is "right in our own eyes." We have to filter all of our thoughts, emotions *and actions* through the lens of Scripture. Being sincere or "true to our nature" don't justify behaviors the Bible has clearly defined as offensive to God.

Lord, may You search our hearts and minds, correcting and guiding us into all truth. Father, we submit our entire lives, our whole hearts and our every desire under Your authority today. Amen.

You brought my life up from the pit,
Oh Lord my God. - Jonah 2:6

The Pit

SOMETIMES LIFE CAN SWIFTLY SLIP AWAY FROM A GLORIOUS mountaintop experience with God into a sudden valley. Into **The Pit.** Maybe you're struggling with it as you read this today, feeling as if life has snatched you up, swallowed you whole and now you're wallowing deep inside it. Surrounded by acid, stench and darkness, there's no mistaking or denying it at this point: you're in **The Pit**.

The Pit is real. It is powerful. But there's also hope.

When we find ourselves in The Pit, we need to pause, look back and review our lives, remembering the many, many times God has brought us through similar pits. Perhaps today's particular pit is deeper or darker than any we've ever experienced. Maybe we're drowning inside, barely able to keep our heads up or catch a breath.

Yet God is faithful, and if you choose to believe that He will bring you through this, you can be assured that there *will* be a time of healing and wholeness. Maybe not tomorrow or even next week, but there *will* come a specific day when you'll finally be able look back on your life — *at this exact moment* — and praise Him for what He did. And on that day you will be able to genuinely and sincerely Thank Him for bringing you out of The Pit.

The Pit *is* real, and it is powerful. You might be in it today or clawing your way out from yesterday, but have faith that one day you will once again find yourself standing on solid ground. Don't give up. Hold to the promise of His faithfulness and you *will* see it!

A good name is more desirable than great riches;
to be esteemed is better than silver or gold. - Proverbs 22:1

A Good Name

Dɪᴅ ʏᴏᴜ ᴋɴᴏᴡ ᴘᴇᴏᴘʟᴇ ᴀʀᴇ ᴛᴀʟᴋɪɴɢ ᴀʙᴏᴜᴛ ʏᴏᴜ?

It's true. Someone is talking about you today.

Okay, maybe they're not talking about you *this very moment*, but it's still true that people talk about you when you're not around. Your name — *you*, specifically — will come up in casual conversations, and you'll never know when or where. It's just a fact of life.

However, what someone else is *saying* about you is somewhat in your control. How so? Because it's all rooted in how you've treated them, how you made them feel. Was your last interaction grounded in love or respect? Anger of frustration? Patience? Forgiveness?

You are in charge of you. How you treat other people, what you say and do is entirely under your control. So whatever impression you're leaving in the world is completely in your hands.

Remember this the next time you have the opportunity to interact with someone else. You're always in the process of leaving a legacy, making a lasting impact. Are you creating a positive one? Or would you say it's been more negative lately? In casual conversations, would your name be considered a good one, or... notsomuch?

It's not about putting on a face, pleasing people or trying to make everybody happy. Establishing a good name is about doing what's good and right and true in our relationships with each other.

Bear with each other and forgive one another
if any of you has a grievance against someone.
Forgive as the Lord forgave you. - Colossians 3:13

The Gift

SOMETIMES WE IMAGINE OUR REFUSAL TO FORGIVE SOMEONE IS a form of punishment for them. We believe it's a way to "make them pay" for how they've offended or hurt us. As if holding onto our unforgiveness would not only validate our own hurt, but somehow cause them to suffer as well. We were wronged, and by not offering forgiveness we think we're making the other person pay a price.

The truth is forgiveness isn't a gift meant for *them*. It's intended for *us*, the wounded ones. Forgiveness gives us the ability to finally let go of an infraction. The freedom and clarity to move forward with our lives, to loosen the weighted shackles around us. Forgiveness is a necessary step to stopping negative, self-destructive emotions such as bitterness, anger and resentment.

When we forgive someone — *whether they deserve our forgiveness or not* — we take the first step toward healing *ourselves*. It is sometimes the most difficult, painful step we can make, but it is positive and it is exceptionally powerful.

Forgiving someone doesn't mean you're expected to forget about what happened or even condone it. Truthfully, you may have to bear the scars of your wounds for longer than you'd expect or want. Instead, forgiveness means you're choosing to open your hands and actively let go of the negative, toxic emotions that are slowly trying to destroy you from the inside out.

The gift for forgiveness isn't about them...

...*it's about you.*

When I called, they did not listen; so when they called,
I would not listen, says the LORD Almighty.
- Zechariah 7:13

The Cost of Ghosting God

HAVE YOU EVER BEEN "GHOSTED" BY SOMEONE? SOMETHING happens between you and a friend, and the next thing you know, they're not answering your calls, texts, e-mails... nothing. You've been ghosted. Ignored. Erased from their day-to-day life.

This passage describes an incredibly depressing picture of both what happened in the past and is prophesied to happen again in the future. God knows our hearts. We may believe we can fool those around us into thinking we're choosing Him, that we're aligned with His purposes and obedient to His voice. But God... God knows our *hearts*. He knows *the truth*. He knows whether we're genuinely following Him or just giving Him lip service when it's convenient or makes us look good.

The Bible says there will come a time in the future when people will once again be praying to God, desperately seeking Him and His help, but they won't find Him. Why not? Because they will not have chosen to hear Him, fear Him and follow Him up to that point, so He will not make Himself available afterwards.

This is a terrifying reality, and it should serve as a wake up call. We can't put off having a serious, committed relationship with God until tomorrow or next week or whenever we feel like it. Because without God's attention and ear — without His omnipresent, sustaining and loving hand of protection — we won't stand a chance.

There is but one God, the Father, from whom
all things came and for whom we live; and there is
but one Lord, Jesus Christ, through whom all things
came and through whom we live. - 1 Corinthians 8:6

The Source

GOD IS YOUR ULTIMATE SOURCE AND SUPPLIER. OFTEN WE'LL define our supplier only by what we directly see or understand, and mistakenly give *them* the authority, praise or worship that rightfully belongs to God.

Your job is not your Source. God has given you the skills and the mind and the opportunity to work, doing what you're doing right now. Sure, your employer provides the checks that you deposit into your bank account, but *they* are not the source.

Your parents are not the source. As a teenager you might have done chores to earn an allowance. Yet your parents were not the source. God is the one who gave them the abundant income they had to be able to share a portion with you. *They* are not the source.

For those in Christian service, it's important we remind ourselves that even our supporters (as loved and appreciated as they are) are not our ultimate source. Yes, they absolutely supply the funds necessary to keep us on the field (*thank you!*), and their prayers and encouragement protects and provides for us in more ways than we'll ever know. But ultimately they are also just stewards of God's blessings, being faithful and obedient to Him in how He guides them. *They* are not the source.

Wherever your income comes from, remember to acknowledge that your ultimate source in this life is God. Jobs will come and go, but the only *true security* you'll experience is when you recognize Him as your provider. Circumstances can change in an instant, but **you can rely on your Heavenly Father as your Source.**

*He gave them no inheritance there, not even enough ground
to set his foot on. But God promised him that he and his
descendants after him would possess the land,
even though at that time Abraham had no child. - Acts 7:5*

Faith without Fruit

WE THINK GOD DOES THINGS LIKE THIS MORE OFTEN THAN WE recognize or realize. He gives us an amazing, mind-blowing promise regarding our future, all while there is absolutely little to no indication in the present that it could ever come to pass. *EVER.*

We mistakenly fix our eyes on the *promise*, while His primary goal is to instill in us greater *faith.* A faith that's strong enough to sustain the setbacks which will discourage us along the way. He wants us to be wholly devoted and trusting of Him *at all times* — not just when we see Him actively working to fulfill the promise.

Some people choose to walk away from God when He doesn't do *what* they wanted, *when* they wanted it to happen. They become so disillusioned and hurt by what they perceive as a betrayal, they abandon Him forever.

Abandonment isn't the only option, of course. We can also choose to *push through* our disappointment and disillusionment about what's happening (or *not* happening). We can choose to worship the one *true* God, as opposed to the On Demand, convenient, comfortable and subservient Genie god many are tempted to believe in.

How about you? Do you believe God's given you a promise? Whispered specific words regarding your future? Have you reached a pivotal moment of disappointment, one where you're tempted to desert Him entirely? Tempted to walk away? To quit?

Don't give up. Please. Ask Him for the encouragement you need to keep holding on, and then pray for the strength to take your next step — *in faith.*

In Him we were also chosen, having been predestined
according to the plan of Him who works out everything
in conformity with the purpose of His will. - Ephesians 1:11

Please Fix This

DOES THIS SOUND FAMILIAR TO YOU? WE ASK GOD TO FIX situations that we feel are threatening to subdue us — even circumstances that are a direct result of our own mistakes. And sometimes He'll do it! Sometimes the Lord will actually intervene and rescue us from our bad decisions. But other times He may instead allow us to feel the full brunt of our poor choices in life.

When we overextend ourselves — whether socially, vocationally, financially or whatever — we can't go running to Him and expect Him to snap and make it all better. He's not going to wave a magic wand just so we don't have to face our consequences. He just isn't.

More often than not, He will opt to walk us *through* those consequences so we can see firsthand His faithfulness in *all* circumstances (whether they were created directly by our own hands or from an external source).

God loves you. He loves you so much more than you could ever grasp or begin to imagine. So don't reduce His love to equate fixing everything in your life so it's always "just right." He loves you too much to do that. He loves us enough to allow our situations to shape us for the future, to help us grow and mature, conforming to His perfect will in our lives.

You can always ask Him for help in life.

Sometimes He'll say yes.

Sometimes He'll say no.

Will you worship Him... regardless?

As the heavens are higher than the earth,
so are my ways are higher than your ways
and my thoughts than your thoughts. - Isaiah 55:9

Unwanted

SOMETIMES WHAT IS BEST FOR US ENDS UP BEING WHAT WE absolutely, positively, do *not* want.

When our family first arrived in **Papua, Indonesia** way back in 2013, **Mission Aviation Fellowship** welcomed us warmly. It was so exciting! The kids were on a high, meeting new friends and playmates, and after many months of delays we had finally arrived at our final destination.

We soon discovered a **Welcome Party** was scheduled for us at 4:00pm that afternoon. This was not good news. After traveling for 48 hours straight, we'd arrived at 6:00am on an overnight flight. We were *already* exhausted, and it was only 6:34 in the morning!

Want to know what a restful trip is not? A restful trip is *not* having kids sleep on your lap (thus preventing *you* from sleeping). It is *not* having stewardesses wake you up at 1:00am (just after you've fallen asleep) to offer you "chicken or fish" for an in-flight dinner that you really, really don't want.

To top it off, I'm an introvert at heart. So the idea of being surrounded by a bunch of new faces, shaking hands and making awkward conversation — all in a sleep-deprived state — sounded like a recipe for social disaster.

Turns out it was exactly what we needed.

You see, not only did we need to meet our new coworkers, but more importantly *we needed to stay awake*. Any global traveller worth their salt will tell you that you must fight to stay awake until 7-8pm your first night to help reset your body clock. Going to bed at 3-4pm in the afternoon is a rookie mistake, resulting in many nights of interrupted, restless sleep.

One day you'll find yourself in a situation you didn't expect and really don't appreciate. You'll want to scream and squirm and protest, but be careful! There's a good chance God has put you exactly where He wants you to be right now. And as uncomfortable as it is, maybe what you're enduring and facing today is specifically designed so He can somehow bless you through it tomorrow.

*The LORD had made the Egyptians favorably disposed
toward the people, and they gave them what they asked for;
so they plundered the Egyptians. - Exodus 12:36*

Take my Gold and Go, Already

HERE'S THE PICTURE: THE EGYPTIANS HAD ENSLAVED THE Israelites for 430 years, and suddenly Moses and Aaron show up and things went from bad to worse.

Moses wasn't excited to go where God was sending him. He knew full well there was little to no hope Pharaoh would ever be willing to let his people go. The guy was an egocentric tyrant. Relenting just wasn't in his nature.

Yet not only did he finally submit and set them free, but God Himself had worked in the hearts of the Egyptian people in such away that they, too, sent the Israelites on their way. In fact, they sent them with all the gold and silver they could find (plus whatever else was requested).

Can you picture that? It's pretty mind-blowing.

What's even more amazing is the fact that God had actually *predicted* this would happen. In *Exodus 3:21-22*, he explained *in detail* that this exact thing would take place.

> And I will make the Egyptians favorably
> disposed toward this people, so that when you
> leave you will not go empty-handed.

We need to remember that it is **God alone** who gives us whatever success and favor we receive in life. *He is the source.* When we trust in Him and His leading, He makes the incredible, the impossible... possible.

You keep track of all my sorrows.
You have collected all my tears in your bottle.
You have recorded each one in your book. - Psalms 56:8 NLT

He May be God...
...But is He Really Good?

IT'S EASY TO WRAP OUR HEADS AROUND GOD'S OMNIPOTENCE. His power is clearly evident in the world around us, both externally and intimately. But when we encounter situations where it appears He's dropped the ball... that's when we start to wrestle with the hard questions. The first and foremost being whether He is *actually* good, a question that becomes even more pronounced when we suddenly lose a loved one.

Emily was one our Dorm Kids over in **Papua, Indonesia**. She was funny and smart, full of laughter and energy and love. She was, by anyone's definition, simply awesome. So when she died in a sudden accident a few years ago, a lot of us were left struggling with some really hard questions.

Why would a loving, all-powerful God choose to take her from us? Why then, of all times? Couldn't He have prevented this in the first place? And if so, then *why didn't He?*

It's not always comforting to hear someone tell you how God is always good. We define His "goodness" as "our comfort" far more often than we'd like to admit it. And when we suffer? Well, that's when His goodness is questioned most of all.

No, it is not always comforting to hear that God is always good... but it *is* true, *regardless* of our feelings.

Emily was gone. We couldn't change that fact. But we could choose how we would to respond to her loss. Run from God and accuse Him of being evil, or run *toward* Him, trusting that He had a reason for this, that absolutely everything has purpose.

What about you? If you haven't already come to a crossroads, know that there will be a time in every believer's life where you will be tempted to dismiss Him. To accuse Him. To reject Him. But you *can* trust Him, believing that He is always and forever will be good, no matter what He allows in life.

*Whoever says, "I know him," but does not do
what he commands is a liar, and the truth is not in that person...
Whoever claims to live in him must live as Jesus did.*

- 1 John 2:4,6

Hugging Discomfort

FAITH IN GOD CAN BE SO FRAGILE SOMETIMES. WITHOUT BEING firmly rooted in the truth of the Bible, our concept of **Who He Is** will quickly become twisted and distorted.

In today's culture it's still surprisingly popular to talk about God. It shouldn't be so shocking, when you think about it. After all, He *has* hardwired eternity in our hearts. We crave and long for a spiritual connection with Him, and yet if most people were honest with themselves, they would quickly admit they really don't want anything to do with the God *of the Bible*.

God? Sure. But the **God of the Bible?** They'll pass.

Instead they want to worship and connect with a god of their own choosing, a more comfortable god of their own design. Forget about righteousness and holiness. Instead let's emphasize this god's attributes of love and acceptance. Hell? Don't even mention it. It's too harsh, too exclusive and uncomfortable, so why believe in it?

Don't fall into this feel-good trap.

God is God, and He does not change.

We should never attempt to box Him in or redefine Him so that we can be more comfortable with Him. If we continue to dilute who He is and what He's about, we'll end up not worshipping Him at all, but a weak, diluted substitute instead.

I press on, that I may lay hold of that
for which Christ Jesus has also laid hold of me. - Philippians 3:12

Stubborn Faith

HERE'S A HARD TRUTH TO RECONCILE ABOUT GOD: HE IS absolutely all-powerful and completely sovereign, and yet He still allows evil things to happen on the earth. He is eternally good, absolutely righteous, incredibly holy, but will permit evil, painful things to happen in our lives.

A common response to God when He leaves our sincere, heartfelt prayers unanswered is to accuse Him. We accuse Him of being callous, or worse, being directly *responsible* for our pain. When He doesn't provide us with acceptable answers in what we believe is a reasonable length of time, we can feel let down. Even betrayed. *"If God loves me so much, if He is really all-powerful and all-knowing, then why doesn't He take this pain away?! Why would He even allow it in the first place?!?"*

Speaking from experience, the only way to get past these overwhelming feelings of betrayal is to foster a **Stubborn Faith**. We must *choose* to not give up, chose to *continue trusting* the same God who has proven Himself faithful to us in the past. We will need a strong, **Stubborn Faith** in our future — a faith for the times when we're unable to see clearly or comprehend how He's working (*or not working*) in our current circumstances.

God is God. He is *not* evil, and He will *never* betray us. Sometimes only time and perspective will prove this truth, but we'll never get there if we don't first choose to believe. Life is going to make you question everything you've ever believed in. Sooner or later, you need to rely on nothing other than your **Stubborn Faith**.

I will give you a new heart and put a new spirit in you;
I will remove from you your heart of stone and give you a heart
of flesh. And I will put my Spirit in you and move you to
follow my decrees and be careful to keep my laws.
- Ezekiel 36:26-27

Hearts of Stone

A HEART OF STONE.

If we didn't know better, we might think this is a good thing. A stone heart means having a *strong* heart, a *protected* heart, a heart that can endure the caustic elements and passing of time to survive.

Yet being strong and protected and self-sufficient is the exact opposite of what God wants from us. Left on our own, we will make every attempt at being self-sustaining. We will steel ourselves to be as strong as possible, stubbornly choosing to do what *we* think is best in every situation. (You kind of have to wonder... is there a *quicker* recipe for disaster than this?)

We need to guard against our heart and its emotional inclinations. Change our prayer focus from our own personal satisfaction and happiness to God's glory and eternal purposes. We are in desperate need of new hearts, in need of replacing the stony ones we drag around day after day with ones that are responsive to His Spirit, receptive to His subtle whispers, to the very Voice of God.

How about your heart? How is it doing today? Would you describe it as soft or pliable? In His trusting hands? Or is it weathered and hardening, desperately trying to protect itself? Is there an area in your life where you feel God's trying to speak into, attempting to soften you? Replacing the stony areas inside with new life?

Jesus answered, "I am the way and the truth and the life.
No one comes to the Father except through me." - John 14:6

The Only Way

WITHOUT QUESTION, BY TODAY'S CULTURAL STANDARDS OF inclusiveness and inoffensive statements, Jesus would be branded incredibly, inexcusably intolerant.

In a world where almost anything goes and "How dare you tell me I'm wrong!" attitudes, Jesus would've made many enemies. For someone to be so bold, so utterly narrow-minded and limiting when it comes to spirituality... well... it would be considered the height of arrogance. But is it arrogant if it's also the truth?

If you loudly proclaim that the sky is blue, is that arrogant? Maybe. If someone's ignorant of the color in the sky they might very well be offended with your narrow view of it. Who are you to say it's not green or red or purple? But all it takes is one glance to verify whether or not it's actually the truth.

Jesus' intention wasn't to be offensive, but He was unapologetic when it came to being absolutely exclusive. **Jesus *is* exclusive.** Aside from Him, there is no other way for us to step beyond the shadow of our sins and come into the presence of the Father. To say otherwise might be "considerate" or "sensitive" or "inclusive," but none of that matters if it's not The Truth. When people are dying in their sins, condemned to eternal separation from God, being inclusive can be damning.

Please. If you haven't prayed the prayer, don't wait:

Jesus, I confess that I am a sinner and I do need your help! I confess that I've chosen myself and what I want rather than what You do. I admit now that I can't be right without you, can't be united with God without you. I believe you are the Son of God and that you actually did die for me. So please, come into my heart today and change me, from the inside out. Amen.

When Jesus reached the spot, he looked up
and said to him,"Zacchaeus, come down immediately.
I must stay at your house today." - Luke 19:5

Detours

WHEN YOU LOOK AT THE GOSPELS, IT'S CLEAR THAT JESUS WAS A pretty busy guy. Always on the move, jetting from place to place, he was constantly teaching to ever-expanding groups of people. Yet even when he was surrounded by the surging crowds, he took time out to *be* with people, intimately.

This was exactly what happened when Jesus went to Jericho. Walking along with the crowd, he suddenly stopped, looked up at Zacchaeus and called him by name. We can sometimes be so laser-focused in life, scrambling to accomplish everything we feel is incredibly, utterly important. So focused, unfortunately, that we lose sight of what's truly valuable. We begin to view people — the crowd around us — as distractions, hindrances... obstacles.

If this sounds familiar to you, it's not too late to change. You can choose to shift your viewpoint today. Life is messy, and people make it more so. (They do.) But life is also beautiful, and often it's *because* of those very same people who make it so messy for us.

Chances are good you're going to face a setback, detour or distraction this week. When you do, ask the Lord to help you see those around you clearly and with new eyes. Then pray to Him, asking for the power to love them by sharing with them what only you can give: your invaluable time and your undivided attention.

For God has not given us a spirit of fear and timidity,
but of power, love, and self-discipline. - 2 Timothy 1:7

For the Hopeless One

ELIJAH WAS A GREAT PROPHET OF GOD. HE'S ONE OF THOSE characters of the Bible who stands out for his radical faith. Yet Elijah was human just like we are, struggling with the same emotions we do — the same fears, the same depression, the same loneliness.

After raising a boy from the dead, being fed by ravens, winning a spiritual showdown against the prophets of Baal and seeing God answer a prayer for rain after a long drought, Elijah was suddenly threatened by Queen Jezebel. So what did he do? He freaked out. It says, *"Elijah was afraid and fled for his life."* (*1 Kings 19:3*)

Have you ever felt like your fears were trying to stop you from fully trusting God? You're in good company. If Elijah can give in to his fear after all of the miraculous signs *he* had experienced firsthand, then obviously fear is something *any* of us can be overwhelmed by.

"I have zealously served the Lord God Almighty," Elijah *wailed. "But the people of Israel have broken their covenant with you, torn down your altars, and killed every one of your prophets. I am the only one left, and now they are trying to kill me, too."*

Fear. Discouragement. Loneliness. *Hopelessness.* We're in good company, aren't we? Amazingly, God didn't respond to Elijah with frustration or pity, but instead recognized that the greatest need he had at the time was *hope.*

We are not alone in our pain. We have a God we can cry out to and openly express our doubts, our fears, our pain and our hopelessness. We serve a Heavenly Father who intimately knows our hearts and minds, and understands our weaknesses. In the middle of our hopelessness, He's willing and able to come to us, reaching down and infusing us with our greatest need: **Hope.**

He took him outside and said, "Look up at the sky
and count the stars — if indeed you can count them."
Then he said to him, "So shall your offspring be." - Genesis 15:5

Numerous

I'LL BE HONEST: I'M NOT MUCH OF A CAMPER OR AN outdoorsman. I'm much more comfortable in air conditioning, reading a book or listening to music than I'll ever be setting up a tent or starting a campfire from scratch. Closest I ever got to being a Cub Scout was when I joined Indian Guides and took on the name "Chief Five Cents." (*Don't ask me why, it just seemed to appeal to my eight-year-old mind at the time...*)

So you can hopefully understand how, despite every opportunity, I never really took much notice of the night sky. City life effectively prevented me from getting an accurate view of the magnitude above me. It wasn't until I moved to Papua, Indonesia, that I had my first eye-opening glimpse.

I was standing outside one evening when the power went out, instantly bathing the neighborhood in complete and utter darkness. It was so thick it was practically tangible. I looked around me for a few seconds and then glanced up, actually gasping at what I saw.

Unhindered by the ambient glow of the city lights, the sky above was crystal clear and completely *swarming* with stars. It was then that I realized we are but specks on this planet, drifting in expansive space, absolutely awash with stars.

Abraham was focused. He knew what he wanted, but his faith began to wrinkle and wither as time passed. After a while, he began to question whether God's promise of a son would ever happen. So God took him outside and gave him a proper perspective, a new outlook on the situation.

It worked. In less than a few seconds, *everything changed.*

Abraham had big dreams. *A son!* A miracle in and of itself! A descendant to carry on the family name and heritage. But God's plans were so far *above* what he was dreaming or hoping for. They were so much bigger *and* infinitely better.

Has God ever given you a promise? A word of encouragement or hope that you once claimed, but now find it harder and harder to cling to? Don't give up hope. Ask Him to give you a fresh perspective today, so you can see His plan *through His eyes*, and why it will be worth the wait.

Let not your hearts be troubled.
Believe in God; believe also in me. - John 14:1

Dead Ends

IT'S EASY TO TRUST GOD WHEN THINGS ARE GOOD.

He'll give us just enough light in our faith walk to keep us from getting too discouraged, enough illumination for the path He's led us to embark on up until now. But what about when the twists and turns along the way don't lead to the land you were promised? What do you do when the dark alley He specifically directed you to enter ends with a brick wall? A dead end?

Will you collapse in an emotional heap? Succumb to the discouragement and disillusionment of your present setback? Maybe shake your fist at Him, curse yourself for being so trusting and believing in His promises in the first place?

There's another option, of course.

You can choose faith. **You can choose to believe.**

You can believe He is *still* good.

He knows where you are, of course. He sees you. Right now.

And as much as it feels like you're forgotten and utterly alone and completely abandoned, please hear me when I say that you are exactly where you're supposed to be right now. This situation isn't a mistake on His part *or yours.*

He always has a reason for every single step you've taken, a reason for every detour, every delay along the way. But you won't see it if you give up or if you surrender to the shadow of sorrow that's trying to overwhelm you.

Don't give up. *Please.*

Choose to believe, to trust in His timing and His reasons. Maybe He'll reveal them to you in this lifetime, maybe the next, but one day you *will* know the *Why.*

But some of them said, "Could not he who opened the eyes
of the blind man have kept this man from dying?" - John 11:37

Where Was God?!?

"GOD, WHERE ARE YOU?"
   "Lord, you're all-powerful! Why didn't you...?"
   "Jesus, you should have done something to stop this!"
   "I'm so angry and hurt! Just when I needed Him the most, I feel
like God completely abandoned me!"

When we don't get what we pray for, it's easy to second-guess God.
We can be so quick to accuse Him of not caring, of ignoring us or
even being flat-out cruel.

How quickly we forget that He is the same at all times —
yesterday, today and forever. He is good, and loving and just, so we
can assume that any answer He provides (or *doesn't* provide) to our
prayers will always be in line with His character.

He sees absolutely everything — the present *and* the future.

Unbelief is easy.

Trust is hard.

Faith is hard.

Maybe what you're going through today feels like it's too much,
like it's too incredibly overwhelming for you right now. Your pain and
anger and confusion are doing their best to strangle you, attempting
to smother the flickering flame of life out of you.

Please don't give up yet.

You can make it through this. Push through your pain and doubt
and fear and grab hold of your faith in Him again. He is still good,
He's still loving and He's still just. He always will be. (Even if you
can't see it in the moment.)

Do not be deceived: God cannot mocked,
whatever one sows, that will he also reap. - Galatians 6:7

The Reaper

WE THINK WE'RE SO SMART.

We can get pretty good at hiding our secret sins. Sure, some of them are out in the open, for all the world to see. Pride, self-centeredness, greed... these are practically on full parade every time we open our mouths. But the inner ones — the thoughts and feelings we stuff down deep, hiding from the world while we cherish and nourish them in our spare time — *those* are the real dangers.

Sins grow and flourish just like seeds. They don't just spring up out of nowhere. They each have a dark, twisted root buried beneath them which has been growing in the soil of our souls for a long, long time, well before their evidence becomes visible.

If we're serious about living lives for Christ, lives marked by righteousness and purity, then we can't ignore these seeds of sin in our lives. We need to be willing to get our hands dirty. Reaching down and digging deep, grabbing hold and uprooting each and every one of them before they sprout up and try to destroy our lives.

Father, please help each of us as we turn over the soil of our souls, identifying and extracting the seeds of sin before they can grow to choke the life out of us.

We continually ask God to fill you
with the knowledge of his will through all the wisdom
and understanding that the Spirit gives. - Colossians 1:9

Wise Guys

WE ALL WANT TO BE SELF-RELIANT, TO FEEL COMPETENT, smart. No matter what vocation we end up in — leading a global mission ministry to editing novels to raising a handful of energetic kids — we all have one thing in common: we want to be in control. We all want to believe that we not only know exactly what we're doing at any given moment, but we can manage it all by ourselves, thank you very much.

It's one thing to be confident in the skills and talents God has given us. This is perfectly normal and encouraged. But confidence becomes conceit when we swell with personal pride, refusing to take outside advice.

As we face life's problems and struggles, we often forget to take advantage of God's wisdom or input. We get so caught up in the moment that it never occurs to us to pause, to call on or ask Him for a fresh influx of insight.

God wants more for us.

The Lord wants us to experience lives of excitement and genuine fulfillment, for us to live lives filled with electrifying *purpose*. But this kind of life is only available when we're willing to relinquish the headstrong belief that we know what's best all the time. When we're open to hearing His voice, He will lead us to unanticipated areas of blessings we never even knew existed.

If we endure, we will also reign with him.
If we disown him, he will also disown us;
if we are faithless, he remains faithful,
for he cannot disown himself. - 2 Timothy 2:12-13

Disowned

WE RECENTLY CAME ACROSS AN ARTICLE THAT SHARED A sobering reality. More and more believers in the future will end up compromising core biblical values and standards, rather than risk being stigmatized, persecuted or "unliked."

Unfortunately, we think it's the truth.

That word — "persecution" — is key. When it comes to clinging to Christ and the Bible vs. getting people to "like" a post or status on social media, more and more people will choose to remain quiet about their faith than take a stand. They will lower their heads, staying silent, and that's extremely saddening.

Staying silent is safe, and staying safe makes sense... if your identity is rooted in what other people think about you. If you only want to be liked in this world and never offend a soul, then keeping your lips zipped is your ultimate goal.

If you're a Christian, however, this isn't an option. Because if you truly believe in Jesus and what the Bible says, you have to be willing to share your beliefs with other people — publicly *or* privately. If you sincerely believe the Bible is a source of Hope and Life to a world that is increasingly hopeless and dying, you will speak up.

The Bible says there will be a time in the future when many believers will abandon their faith to please the world. Sadly, when you look at the world around us, it's hard not to recognize this time is drawing closer and closer to us with every passing day.

Don't be afraid. Cling to Him, and He will prove Himself to be faithful in your life — no matter *what* kind of persecution you may have to face. **Speak truth, always!**

"Many will say to Me in that day, 'Lord, Lord,
have we not prophesied in Your name, cast out demons
in Your name, and done many wonders in Your name?'
And then I will declare to them,
'I never knew you; depart from Me." - Matthew 7:22-23

A Holy Idol

WHEN WE THINK OF IDOLS, WE RARELY ASSOCIATE THEM WITH
the concept with holiness. Greed? Pride? Lust? Sure, those are easily
identifiable idols. So it might come as a surprise to hear that our
pursuit of holiness can also become an idol if we're not careful.

The idol of holiness, like *any* idol, keeps us in bondage to rules.
We mistakenly think we need to perform or act a certain way to get a
predictable result. But life isn't about how well we pursue purity or
holiness, but how well we respond to God's pursuit of *us*.

If someone asks you about your relationship with God, you'd
probably interpret this to mean they're asking if you have a regular
quiet time, moments set aside to pray to Him or read the Bible. Yet
spending time with God and actually loving Him aren't necessarily
the same thing. The degree to which we trust and communicate with
Him are not always contingent on how quiet we are in His presence,
nor the amount of time we devote to Him.

Jesus' statement "I never knew you" is humbling. Sobering.
Terrifying, if we're being completely honest. Yet it reminds us of the
importance of our need to actually pursue Him, intimately allowing
Him to speak into our hearts, rather than learning about Him and
relegating Him to cold facts and head knowledge. Despite everything
else that vies for our attention in our lives, discovering and loving
God for who He truly is should be the base upon which we build all
our other projects and goals.

In all this, Job did not sin
by charging God with wrongdoing. - Job 1:22

Charging God

WHEN FACED WITH DISAPPOINTMENT IN GOD, MANY OF US struggle with knowing how to respond. The typical scenario is we've prayed long and hard for something specific, genuinely *believing* God was leading us or moving in a certain direction, but then everything goes sideways. We're left empty and confused, disillusioned and crushed. Instead of holding a victory, we're left holding a bag of our hurt, our anger and our bitterness... at *Him*.

In times like these, we need to remember what happened to Job. In *a single day*, and due to no fault of his own, he lost almost everything he valued: his property and wealth, his sons and daughters, even his good reputation. One day it was there, the next it was all ripped out of his hands.

Yet even in the face of such calamity, he steadfastly *refused* to hate God. Instead, he humbly accepted and respected God's right to do whatever He chose to do with his life. He could have balled his hands into fists, shaking them at the Lord in angry accusations, but rather he lowered himself even further, hands open in simple surrender to the God in Heaven.

We've all seen it. Good, faith-filled men and women around us turning bitter because of unanswered prayers, withering under their disillusionment with God. Sadly, it's only human to turn against Him for not getting our way. Yet the Bible makes it clear that when we *accuse* God of something, we're essentially saying He is *not* good. And that *is* a sin.

Thankfully, there's a better way. Instead of pulling away, we should take our disappointment and pain and turn *toward* God. When we are crushed we need to remember that He loves and is for us *always* — no matter what happens (or *doesn't* happen) in response to our prayers.

Have you ever felt let down by God? After the disappointment, did you come to Him with faith... or with fury? Maybe this is where you're at right now, in the present. If so, will you choose to continue to trust Him, to trust in His divine timing?

*For the accuser of our brothers and sisters,
who accuses them before our God day and night,
has been hurled down. They triumphed over him by the blood of the
Lamb and by the word of their testimony; they did not love their lives
so much as to shrink from death. - Revelation 12:10-11*

Lovers of Life

They did not love their lives so much as to shrink from death.

HOW MANY OF US CAN SAY THIS TODAY? HONESTLY? NOW THAT we're so thoroughly ingrained in social media and getting "likes" and being loved, who among us can truly proclaim that they would not be afraid of losing it all?

The Bible is unquestioningly clear about the cost of our faith in the future. One day there will be a time — most likely in our lifetime — when identifying ourselves as a Christian will come at a great cost. Economic hardship, social persecution, perhaps even death itself.

Jesus tells us that if we hold fast and are willing to testify about Him before man, He will testify on our behalf before God in Heaven. He is the Advocate we desperately need.

May we all commit right now to remain strong and steadfast in our faith. To be so deeply grounded, so richly rooted in Him that we will never, *ever* deny him.

Lord, help us all. Let us not cherish our present lives — which are but passing breaths, mere mists twisting in the wind — so much that we forfeit eternity itself.

For it is not those who hear the law who are righteous
in God's sight, but it is those who obey the law
who will be declared righteous. - Romans 2:13

Sincerely, Clueless

IT'S NOT ENOUGH FOR US TO HEAR THE TRUTH. PEOPLE TALK about "truth" all day long — on TV or radio, in the news or in conversations on social media. Everybody is always acting on what they believe truth to be. The problem with our belief in truth — regardless of how sincere we feel about it — does *not* mean whatever we believe in is, in fact, **true**.

Example: I am free to *sincerely believe* that I can scoop up a puffer fish from the ocean and take a bite out of it without suffering severe consequences (such as a prolonged and painful death, for instance). Now, *regardless of how sincere I am in my belief*, that would sincerely be a really bad, terrible, no good idea.

The Bible is clear that even the demons believe in Jesus. Does this make them Christians? Of course not. Christians show their *belief* in Jesus by *acting* on their faith. It's not enough to read or listen to the Word, passively hearing the truth it contains. **We must also act on it.** Hearing a sermon about Jesus' love and sacrifice *will not save us*. It won't. It is only when we act on our belief — actively asking Him to forgive us for our sins and make us holy and blameless before a righteous God — that we will be saved.

Jesus is the only way. Do not equate your extensive or detailed knowledge *about* Him for actually having a relationship *with* Him. Knowing *about* Him is great, but it won't save you. Salvation only happens when you combine what you hear with how you live, when you choose to *know Him* and *follow Him*.

In addition to all this, take up the shield of faith, with which
you can extinguish all the flaming arrows of the evil one.
— Ephesians 6:16

A Graceful Reminder

WE DON'T KNOW ABOUT YOU, BUT WE DON'T ALWAYS DO everything right. Sure, we try to, but inevitably we're going to mess up at some point. It's a part of life. Making mistakes — small and large — is part of being human.

We need to remind ourselves that not only are we imperfect, but we're also not *expected* to be perfect. We were not *created* to be perfect. So when we keep putting extra pressure on ourselves to be better or do more, it's bound to spill over into our other relationships.

This is a specially true for those of us who are perfectionists, the ones who hold higher expectations for their immediate family and friends. Inevitably, they will all let us down in some way or another, but how we *react* to these moments of disappointment is crucial.

In the same way that we, ourselves, have received patience and grace from God, we also need to extend this same measure of grace to others. It's perfectly alright to have expectations for behavior, but don't be so married to those high ideals that you inadvertently crush someone's spirit when things go wrong. (And they *will* go wrong...)

Breathe. Take some time to get in the right frame of mind, regaining whatever perspective you might have lost, and treat others the way you would want to be treated.

Gracefully.

Anyone who claims to be in the light
but hates a brother or sister is still in the darkness.
- 1 John 2:9

In Darkness

HAVE YOU EVER FOUND YOURSELF IN THE DARK?

Over in Indonesia, blackouts are fairly common events. You could be having a casual dinner with friends at one moment, and a second later the power goes out and you're all plunged into complete and utter darkness. It makes eating your next forkful an exciting challenge, for sure.

As Christians, we can't claim to love Jesus and desire to follow His word and His ways while simultaneously nursing a grudge against someone else. We can't proclaim how we want the Holy Spirit to oversee every area of our lives during the day, while secretly wishing or praying for something bad to happen to someone else at night. As long as there's a contradiction, any forward spiritual growth is completely stalled.

If we say we're followers of Christ but harbor hatred and unforgiveness in our hearts — *regardless of how righteous or justified we feel about it* — we are going to spend a very long time walking around in the darkness.

Stop stumbling around in the dark.

Ask God for help in extending forgiveness to those who have wronged you. Forgive, remembering how much the Lord has already forgiven you in your own life.

The Lord answered Moses, "Is the Lord's arm too short?
Now you will see whether or not
what I say will come true for you." - Numbers 11:23

Too Short?

IN THIS PASSAGE, MOSES WAS OVERWHELMED AT THE ISRAELITE people's complaining. They complained there was nothing to *eat*, and God gave them manna. Then they complained they didn't have any *meat*, so God supernaturally sent them quail.

However, sometimes it's the very things that we are earnestly wanting and desperately praying for that can become a curse in itself. In this instance, God told them upfront that He would grant their relentless requests, but they would end up having have so much meat to eat that it would "come out of their nostrils."

That's quite a visual. Meat... out of nostrils. *Ick.*

At this point even Moses himself expressed his skepticism, and wondered where all of this magical meat was going to come from. He theorized that even if all the fish in the sea were caught, would it amount to being enough for them?

We might feel removed from the story, but are we much different? We complain about our situation and ask God to change it, "no matter what." Even if God tells us what He's going to do, do we accept Him at His word, or do we nitpick over the *how* and *when* of it all?

God's answer to Moses is perfect. Is His arm too short to make these things happen? Is He *not* capable? Why, after all the miracles they had experienced up to that point, were they questioning the Creator of *everything*? Their divine Deliverer?

Lord God, Dear Father in Heaven, please help us learn how to hold our tongues during our own personal situations of doubt. Help us remain silent and maintain a stubborn faith, so we might witness Your love and faithfulness firsthand.

Do not pay attention to every word people say, or you may hear
your servant cursing you — for you know in your heart
that many times you yourself have cursed others.
- Ecclesiastes 7:21

Can't Please Everyone

SOLOMON'S WORDS ARE ESPECIALLY INTRIGUING FOR US TODAY, living in the information age. Now is the time when we commonly know someone's strong opinions *before* we know their hearts. We can be easily side-tracked into seeking the approval of people around us here below, rather than the approval of our Father in Heaven.

Solomon keyed into a liberating truth: we can't make everyone happy. We're going to fail and disappoint each other from time to time. *All of us.* As much as we want people to like us and understand us, someday we're going to step on someone else's feet, saying something inappropriate (or outright stupid), or making a decision that's unpopular. It's not our job to make people happy, but we still get sidetracked when we think others might be upset with us.

When it comes to criticism, how can we learn to separate words that need to roll off our backs from the ones that can wisely turn us toward the truth?

We must focus firmly on what is *most* important. We've not been called to make people happy, but to *love* them — even when it hurts. By staying grounded about what *is* important, we're better able to eliminate the things that are *not*. Self, ego, pride, longing for success, desire for respect... these are the distractions, the false gods we believe are worth of our time, but aren't.

Don't let yourself get too caught up in other people's opinions of you, or you'll be entangled in them for the rest of your life. Be strong, be considerate, and go do whatever it is God's calling you to do in life. *Regardless* of whether other people may or may not approve.

So don't be anxious about tomorrow.
God will take care of your tomorrow too.
Live one day at a time. — Matthew 6:34 (TLB)

Happy, now?

HAPPINESS DOES NOT COME EASILY. SO OFTEN WE THINK OUR happiness is rooted in our specific circumstances, when the reality couldn't be further from the truth. Think about it: if our circumstances were the sole cause of our happiness (or unhappiness, as the case may be), then we would be happy *all the time*.

Why? Because we could constantly change our circumstances to accommodate our ever-changing moods, boosting them from lows to highs on a whim.

Unfortunately, life doesn't work like this. Happiness is more of a state of mind than a place or circumstance. Sometimes we think we have to examine our past or uncover painful memories to somehow "get happy," but excessively thinking about our past (or whatever we think our problems are) only serves to convince us that we have great reasons to be *unhappy today*.

All you have is today.

All you have is this very moment, *right now*.

When you stop focusing on the problems of the past or worrying about the potential ones in the future, you'll be able to focus on everything that is *right in your life* — right here, right now, in this present moment.

There is so much that God has given you, so much that you can be happy and thankful for. Don't let yourself be blinded to it by getting caught up in everything that's trying to distract you and drag you down.

Do not be in a hurry
to leave the king's presence.
- Ecclesiastes 8:3

Don't Rush Him

THE TEMPTATION TO RUSH OUR LIVES IS EVER-PRESENT.

Unless we're intentionally resisting the urge, we will tend to rush in most everything we want to do. We will be in a rush to get to this appointment, accomplish that task or achieve the next goal. We pack our schedules to the brink, barely leaving any room for margin.

If we manage to make time for God at all, we're often shortening it prematurely to better accommodate the expanding list of *other* things we want to get to.

Sound familiar? Maybe it's time to reprioritize.

Life is *never* going to naturally slow down. It just isn't. So if we want to get off the merry-go-round and actually breathe, we're going to have to be intentional about it. Downshifting can either happen because we *make* it happen, or because a breakdown requires it.

As you study the Bible, you'll find time and time again that God is not one to rush. He is patient and intentional in everything He does. Even if we're quick to define His timing as "late" today, one day we will see in hindsight that it was all absolutely, inarguably perfect.

Don't try to rush God.

Give Him Time.

He knows what He's doing with your life. Really.

In the same way you judge others, you will be judged,
and with the measure you use, it will be measured to you.
- Matthew 7:2

Measured

THERE IS A DIRECT CORRELATION BETWEEN WHAT WE GIVE AND what we get in this life. *Money, love, grace, mercy...* it all comes back to us, and usually in larger and greater quantities than what we originally doled out.

Depending on what we're giving, many of us absolutely *love* this idea. When we think about the number of positive things we could get in the future, it makes us grin, right? But we don't want to believe in concepts like reciprocation and multiplication when we consider the negative things we give to those around us, do we?

Hatred, unforgiveness, resentment, gossip...

So maybe it's time we sat down and honestly asked ourselves: what have we been extending to the people in our lives lately? Forgiveness? Grace? A little extra patience?

Or... is it something else?

But we continue to preach
because we have the same kind of faith
that the psalmist had when he said,
"I believed in God, so I spoke." - 2 Corinthians 4:13

Encourage one another daily,
as long as it is called "today." - Hebrews 3:13

Wanted: 100% Humans

SOMETIMES WE MAY FEEL LIKE WE NEED TO KNOW ALL THE answers before we talk to someone else about God. As if we have to be some kind of theological giant, ready to quote any and all scripture at a moment's notice.

Turns out, that's kind of ridiculous.

Why? Because it doesn't take an advanced degree in theology or to be perfectly fluent in Christianese for us to be willing to share our faith. We can be 100% honest with each other when it comes to God, *even if* we still have a handful of doubts, niggling questions or more than a few fears or serious struggles.

People will be more interested in knowing what we believe if they recognize that we're human too. In fact, our humanity — saved by grace — can encourage others to have stronger faith as a result. But it all starts with being open, honest and transparent.

So maybe you don't know everything about everything. And no, you may not always get all the answers right when people have questions. Don't let this stop you. You are still free to share what you *do* know! Is today still called "today"? Yes? Then find someone out there who needs a word of encouragement and share what little faith you have in hand! (Regardless of how small or insignificant it may appear in your own eyes...)

If it is possible, as far as it depends on you,
live at peace with everyone.
- Romans 12:18

Make It Right

EVERYBODY MAKES MISTAKES.

Sometimes those mistakes are small, solved by a relatively easy fix. Other times our mistakes are gigantic, absolutely monstrous, and the fallout from them can affect us for years, decades or quite possibly the rest of our lives.

Despite what you've done (or *haven't* done yet), it is never too late to do the right thing. You might not be able to make things right. You probably can't prevent what's already been set into motion. This doesn't mean you're frozen in place, trapped in a hopeless state.

If you're reading this, the good news is you're still breathing. So as long as you're still alive and kicking, you can still choose to do what you need to do to try and start repairing the damage, working to bridge the gap between you and those on the other side.

No matter what's happened, there is always *something* that you, personally, can do to try to set things right again. Make the apology. (Or two. Or three...) Seek forgiveness. Confess. (*Everything!*) Yes, there's always a chance you might not get the response you're hoping or praying for, but you will finally be able to find rest for your soul, knowing you've done everything in your power to introduce peace into your relationship again.

And he swore by him who lives forever and ever,
who created the heavens and all that is in them,
the earth and all that is in it, and the sea and all that is in it,
and said, "There will be no more delay!"
- Revelation 10:6

Wait for it...

WE'RE ALWAYS GOING TO BE WAITING FOR SOMETHING.

Waiting in line, waiting for dinner to come out of the microwave, waiting for a response to our calls, our letters, our e-mails or voicemails. We don't like waiting, but we also know it's just a part of life. Yet did you recognize the common theme in these examples?

They all revolve around us.

Waiting is essentially egocentric, orbiting in and out of our perception of time. It's so incredibly us-focused that it's downright embarrassing, when you really think about it.

So why should we be so surprised to recognize there's a waiting period built into prayer? Because — like so many other things in our lives — we think they all revolve around us. *Our* prayers, *our* desires, *our* needs. With this kind of an approach to prayer, is it any wonder we're frustrated and impatient with getting "the answers we want"?

Prayer is about trust, more than anything else. It's about not only trusting that God is there, but that He is absolutely good and is in control of this crazy world (even this year). Then it's about *maintaining* that trust — *that faith* — **even when** things don't happen the way *we* think they should. (*Especially* when they don't...)

Your perspective is the key. You don't have to be discouraged or disillusioned if you don't want to be. He loves faith, and will give you ever opportunity to offer it to Him. He wants to know if you're still going to trust in Him, trusting in His timing... even if you think He's running late.

*The seeds on rocky ground are those who hear the word
and receive it with joy, but they have no root. They believe
for a season, but in the time of testing, they fall away.*
- Luke 8:13

Blueprint Not Included

SOME PEOPLE WANT TO WORSHIP A GOD WHO'S EASY TO understand. One who won't let life spin out of control too often, or will at least give the reins back to them when it does so they can fix it all. But the God of the Bible? Well, to put it bluntly, He's more interested in fostering our faith than He is in giving us a nice, comfortable blueprint of our future.

We are so very, very human, and our faith can be so very, very fickle at times. How quickly we'll shift our focus on the pressing, insurmountable obstacles of today, completely forgetting the miracles He provided us yesterday.

Far too many Christians approach church and faith as if it were some kind of glorified country club, a holy social outlet or family substitute. If they were honest with themselves, they'd admit they don't really know what they believe, what the Bible really says or who Jesus really is. They just want to feel "included."

My prayer is that God will reveal Himself in all of our lives in a direct, personal way. Breaking through our wall of objections and distractions in a method that's so profound and mind-blowing, that when our shallow beliefs are later challenged by life (*the world, etc.*) we'll be able to not only survive, but will **stand firm**.

Every good and perfect gift is from above.
- James 1:17

Today

TODAY IS ALL WE HAVE.

Today is all we've been given. This moment, *right now*. Yet most of us can hardly enjoy it because our focus is typically elsewhere. Many of us are constantly caught up in a past regret, preoccupied by something that was said or done (either *by* us or *to* us), and we keep replaying it in our minds — stuck in a perpetual, endless loop.

On the other end of the spectrum, we may find ourselves desperately clinging to the hope for a better future, a tomorrow where the worries and stresses of today are somehow nonexistent. We romanticize it, thinking "if only" we had more money / time / friends / *(fill-in-the-blank)* **then** our lives would be perfect and we could *finally* slow down and enjoy ourselves.

Or we may be in perpetual motion, always in a hurry to **Get Things Done**. We link busyness to productivity, and productivity to self-worth. If people see how very busy we are, then perhaps they'll consider us worthy. Valuable. Important. Finally "good enough." If we could only work a little harder, just a bit faster or more efficiently, we'd somehow get ahead and *then* have the time to finally relax.

Taking the time to slow down and actually live life isn't something we should put off until tomorrow or next week. All we have is *now*. Yesterday is gone, tomorrow isn't even real, but today? Today is *here*, in our hands right *now*, and it is the *only* time that we are ever guaranteed.

Life — *real life* — is taking place all around us, whether we recognize it or not. We could all use a few moments to readjust our focus and ask God to show us the incredible gift He has *already* given to us: **Today.**

Come boldly to the throne of our Gracious God.
There we will receive His Mercy and we will find
grace to help us when we need it. - Hebrews 4:16

Approaching God

As children of God, we have constant and instant access to the **King of Kings**, the **Lord of Lords**, our **Heavenly Father**. Whenever the time and whatever our needs, He is available and His full attention is devoted to us. The more often we come into His presence, the more comfortable and natural we become around Him. The more we understand who He is and the extent of His incredible grace toward us, the more we'll feel the freedom to come boldly into His presence.

We should always approach Him with reverence and respect, of course, without losing sight that He is also our loving Heavenly Father who cares for us and delights in having fellowship with us. We can enter into His presence with a relaxed and joyful heart in the assurance that God loves us more than anyone else has loved us up to this point or will ever love us in the future.

God genuinely desires our fellowship and intimacy. He desires to be *with* us. Because of Jesus' sacrifice on the cross, we have unparalleled access to the Creator of the Universe. God has made available to us His vast resources of power, wisdom, love and grace, if only we're willing to surrender to Him, trust Him and obey Him.

Honest, intimate prayer is simply communicating with God, inviting Him to speak into your life as you place your world into His hands. You don't have to present perfectly crafted words or a choreographed approach... just come to Him.

God loves you today, right now, *just as you are.*

He wants to spend time with you.

Spend a few minutes in His presence again today, letting Him know your heart. He is there, listening and loving.

"You cannot serve God and wealth."
- Luke 16:13

Stuffed

Wealth - an abundance of valuable possessions or money.

THE GREEK WORD USED FOR WEALTH IS MAMONIA, WHICH IN older translations is rendered as "mammon."

When we hear the word "wealth" we typically associate it with the possession of money, but *mammon* is far more inclusive. *Mammon* essentially describes the collection and worship of all of our **STUFF**.

Sure, this includes our money (*savings and checking accounts, retirement funds, investments*), but it's more than that. Mammon also refers to our cars, our houses, our collections, etc.

Basically... **all of our STUFF.**

Jesus says we must all choose — every single one of us — whether we will serve God or our **STUFF**. We're going to end up worshipping one or the other. Each of us will dedicate our time and energy and attention to one or the other. We will submit to one... or we will submit to the other.

Devotion to one produces blessings.

Devotion to the other... does not.

We cannot serve both God and Our Stuff.

"Lord, open his eyes so that he may see."
- 2 Kings 6:17

What's Right with This Picture?

So many times we take stock of our lives and find them lacking. (*Usually after binging on social media for an evening, reading about all the happy people with their happy lives and perfect pictures of food or furry friends or family... you get the idea...*) We start to dip our chins, push out our lower lips and think "What is *wrong* with me? Why can't my life be more like *theirs*?!"

Can we all just take a moment right now and agree that what we see online or on social media is *not* a realistic picture? *All of us* have problems and struggles in our lives and relationships. We do! We just don't post every single depressing detail about them online for the world to see and comment on. (*Well, **most** of us don't, anyway...*)

Instead of focusing on what's *wrong* with your world, ask the Lord to show you **what's right** in it. Ask Him to reveal the truth about your life in this precise slice of time, so you might see what's happening around you *from His perspective*. He is waiting and willing to show you the many things you can be thankful for, or how He's divinely orchestrated blessings into your life. Blessings that you'll never see as long as you're staring at your belly button.

Lift your eyes.

Look up.

See the Truth.

Refocus on what's *right* in your life!

Therefore, there is now no condemnation
for those who are in Christ Jesus,
because through Christ Jesus the law of the Spirit
who gives life has set you free from the law of sin and death.
- Romans 8:1-2

Forgiven and Free

You have been set free from sin.

Hallelujah!

Whatever you did last night, last week, or even a few minutes ago... is in the past. If you've confessed it, turned away from it, cast it away from you for what it is, then thank God, your past is not being held over your head. Christ says you are not guilty!

You are a new creature.

You are not condemned.

You are forgiven.

Listen, God is not angry with you. He's not fuming up in heaven, shaking His head and thinking you stink like moldy cheese. He's not keeping a record of your wrongs, writing down every screw up or holding your past against you.

You are forgiven.

It might be the hardest thing you've had to do in a long time, but maybe it's time for you to forgive yourself. He's not condemning you, so stop crucifying yourself again and again. The sacrifice was already made. Paid in full.

You are His.

You Are Forgiven.

But each person is tempted when they are dragged away
by their own evil desire and enticed.
- James 1:14

Hooked

HAVE YOU EVER HEARD OF A TREBLE HOOK? I'LL BE HONEST AND admit right off that I didn't know what one was until just a few days ago. Based on the name alone, I would've thought it had something to do with songwriting or composing a catchy jingle.

This is far from the truth.

A treble hook is one that has three separate and distinct barbs — each one designed to securely hook and latch onto the target. Regardless of which side embeds itself first, it's pretty nasty stuff.

There's a scene in *Peter Jackson's King Kong* when the gigantic creature bursts out of the jungle and into the village. The sea men flank the entrance, awaiting his arrival, and just as he pushes through the gates they throw gigantic treble hooks at Kong. The barbs sink deep into his flesh, and they begin pulling to weigh him down.

This is the image that comes to mind when I consider the power of negative thoughts in our lives. Individual negative thoughts are rarely effective, but when a bunch of them sink into us at the same time and we're weighed down by our emotions — depression, pessimism, etc. — they can become absolutely debilitating. Before we know it, we're getting tangled up, pulled down by their weight.

It is so important that we filter our thoughts and protect ourselves from negativity. If we don't, we risk being overcome, the barbs sinking under our skin until we're neutralized, immovable and paralyzed.

Look to the Lord and his strength; seek his face always.
Remember the wonders he has done, his miracles.
- 1 Chronicles 16:11-12

Remember The Wonders

WE GET SO CAUGHT UP IN THE HECTIC CHAOS OF LIFE, IT becomes easy for us to forget everything that He's already done for us. It takes a concerted, concentrated effort to take our eyes off of an anxious future and look back at how He's brought us through every trial leading up to today.

Remember. Remember what He's already done in your life and the lives of those around you. Signs of God's incredible faithfulness are everywhere, but we'll miss it if we get caught up in the present and the future. We need to remember.

Return your focus on the miracles that happened yesterday so you can find rest in His providence for tomorrow.

Answer me when I call to you, my righteous God.
Give me relief from my distress; have mercy on me
and hear my prayer... Fill my heart with joy.
- Psalm 4:1,7

Take the Risk

ARE YOU COMFORTABLE RIGHT NOW? MAYBE YOUR FEET ARE propped up as you're sitting in your favorite chair, sipping your preferred warm beverage as you settle into your quiet time with your Bible (and favorite devotional)? Yes?

Let's be honest, life can be pretty uncomfortable. So it shouldn't be a surprise that we spend much of our time, money and resources in pursuit of things that will maximize our comfort. We obsess over getting just the right furniture with the perfect fabric, listening only to our favorite worship songs, eating what we love and writing with our preferred scribbling utensil or our computer of choice. (Yes, we're preaching to ourselves, here...)

The truth is, too much comfort can be a dangerous thing. We become so comfortable with the ordinary, the *familiar*, that we become risk averse. But if we've committed ourselves to following Christ, there will inevitably be times when God wants more of us. He'll ask us to expand our focus beyond the boundaries of what we see, beyond what we know or beyond the borders within which we've become comfortable. He will call us outside our comfort zones.

Make no mistake, when He does this it will feel absolutely terrifying, and our emotions will protest loudly. Yet when we respond to the Father's voice with faith and obedience, He will give us far more than we could ever dream or hope for.

How about you? Do you feel God might be calling you to step out of your comfort zone? And if so, are you ready to trust Him?

One person gives freely, yet gains even more;
another withholds unduly, but comes to poverty.
- Proverbs 11:24

The Lesser Side of More

ON THE SURFACE, GIVING STUFF AWAY DOESN'T SEEM LIKE A surefire way to get more in life. It just doesn't add up. If we **want more**, we're constantly encouraged to **make more** and **save more** and **do more** so we can finally have **more**. Giving **more** away? That just sounds... stupid. Counterintuitive.

So let's look at it from a different angle.

Consider financial investments. If an investor only invests a little bit at a time, their investment's not going to end up very big in the end. Yet if they give generously into the investment, their money's going to produce a good-sized profit in the end.

Everything you have has been given to you. Everything you have was ultimately provided by God, and no, it's not just for your comfy comfort or benefit. So hold it all with loose, open hands. Be willing to give some of it away when you see someone else in need, remembering a time in your own life when you were blessed by someone else's generosity. Heck, be ready to give a huge *chunk* of it away if God's leading you to!

When you give freely, **God has promised to provide abundantly for your every need**. It's not always a cent-for-cent return, but you can rest assured that you *will*, in some way, gain **more** as a result of your generosity.

Maybe it'll come back in the form of money, but maybe it'll show up as time or — best of all — peace of mind. (And let's be honest, which of those three do you want the **most**? Honestly?)

Two are better than one, because they have a good return
for their labor. If either of them falls down,
one can help the other up. But pity anyone who falls
and has no one to help them up. - Ecclesiastes 4:9-10

Mistakes Were Made

As I write these words today, I'm somewhat in a state of shock. A friend — a good, trusted, amazing friend — recently revealed they'd made a terrible mistake. It was enough of a burden that I lost sleep for days following the revelation, laying awake in the night as an endless string of questions arose in my mind...

How could they do this?

What had they been thinking?

Why hadn't they guarded themselves better?

Avoided getting into this situation in the first place?

In the end, there were more questions than answers. Even if they were explored in our conversations, I don't honestly believe the answers would have provided me with a sense of relief or comfort.

It is what it is. It happened. It hurts. But there's nothing that can be done about it now. As much as we both wish we could go back in time and undo what's been done, we can't. We can only move forward, making better choices in the future.

If you've ever faced (or are currently facing) a similar situation in your own life, sometimes the best thing you can do is offer someone a listening ear. Don't minimize the situation, but don't condemn them more than their hearts already are. Pray with them, listen to them, then help them get back on their feet again.

You may be tempted to distance yourself, to pull back out of fear of discomfort. Don't. Don't leave them struck down in the dirt, stuck in the muck. They need a friend now more than ever, someone who will speak truth and life into their lives.

And it is impossible to please God without faith.
Anyone who wants to come to him must believe that God exists
and that He rewards those who sincerely seek Him.
- Hebrews 11:6

Faith First

EVER GOTTEN DISTRACTED IN LIFE WITH YOUR ENDLESS To Do lists? We have so much to do each day, and God has purposed much work *for* us to do. But we don't work in order to please Him. We work in order to share Him with others, as an outpouring of our love for Him and our understanding of His endless love for each of us.

When our work becomes our main focus, however, we start to expect certain responses, rewards or recognition. We look at our various daily disappointments and want to shake our fists in frustration. "But I did all of these things for *you*, Lord!"

Make no mistake, your Father is pleased with faith.

He is pleased by a heart earnestly and openly wanting to find Him and serve Him. He is exceptionally pleased by our patient endurance and confident trust.

But the truth is He doesn't *need* our work and isn't looking to see if we are "good enough" to get His full attention or blessings. Work helps us to grow with each passing day, month and year, but it will never be as valuable or important to Him as our *faith*.

Work is good. It is.

But **faith is better.**

Father, may we not lose our faith as we sort through the ever-shifting mountain of our work.

How long, Lord? Will you forget me forever?
How long will you hide your face from me?
How long must I wrestle with my thoughts
and day after day have sorrow in my heart?
- Psalm 13:1-2

How Long?

DAVID WAS ONE OF A KIND.

Described as a man "after God's own heart," David not only experienced the highs and lows of human emotions, but he was extremely transparent and honest about expressing them. If we've learned anything from the Psalms, it's how God is unafraid of hearing about our struggles, our emotions or our constant questions.

At some point during their lifetime, every Christian will be seriously tempted to walk away from their faith. To turn around, abandon it and not look back. The most common roots of this turning are *pain* and *suffering*. Something terrible happens — either to them or to someone they dearly love — and they just can't reconcile how God could ever create something good out of it.

If this is where you're at right now, please hear us that there *is* hope. The good news is God will never abandon you. Ever. From your perspective in The Pit, however, you may well feel like He's not only forgotten you, but He's actively hiding His face from you. You're wrestling with your faith with everything in you, and maybe you're not even sure if you're going to make it through this time.

If this is where you're at, there's no point denying it. Admit it. Call it for what it is. But don't stop there. If you will *choose* to hold on, *choose* to believe, there will be a day when you'll look back at this moment right here, and nod your head in gratitude, seeing how God miraculously made it all work out for good in the end.

The Lord does not see as man sees;
for man looks at the outward appearance,
but the Lord looks at the heart. - 1 Samuel 16:7

X-Ray Specs

HAVE YOU EVER SEEN A PAIR OF X-RAY GOGGLES ADVERTISED IN the back of a vintage magazine or online? Those were always so intriguing when I was growing up, the notion that I could just slap them on and immediately have X-ray vision! (Sadly, the reality didn't quite live up to the hype.)

We get so caught up with outward appearances, don't we? We're impressed with other people's titles, with prestige and honor. It's one thing to show someone respect, but it is another to defer to or give someone else power or authority based on position alone. Everybody's human, and while some people can appear picture perfect on the outside, like highly polished pots of gold, the inside is another story. The truth begins and resides in our hearts. And God? Well... God sees *everything*.

It's important that we keep everything in perspective. Our esteem for others, our self-respect, our hearts. Whatever's inside is going to come out anyway, whether through words or actions. So the sooner we purify our hearts, the better we'll be — both inside *and* out.

What do you think God sees when He looks at your heart?

Does He see someone devoted to Him and to the things of His kingdom? Or someone devoted to themselves and their own comfort and security? Is there something you feel He wants to change in your own heart this week?

Above all, love each other deeply,
because love covers over a multitude of sins.
- 1 Peter 4:8

Humans

HAVE YOU NOTICED THIS WORLD IS JUST *FULL* OF HUMANS?

Walking, talking, feeling, living, breathing *humans*.

And that's not all. These humans have the potential to be mean-spirited, hurtful, selfish, downright cruel and sometimes just plain nasty. Now, if you somehow haven't met such a human yet, don't worry... you will.

Oh yes, this world is chock-full of humans. Humans who make mistakes. Humans who heal the world. Who hurt each other. Who use their God-given minds to create... or destroy.

For better or worse, *this* is humanity.

While it's easy to see the glaringly obvious faults of those around us (*especially those closest to us*), we need to remember that we, too, are so very, very human. And just as we need to extend forgiveness to those who have wronged us, there will come a day when we will also be in need of receiving it.

Contrary to what you've probably heard or been told, forgiveness isn't a feeling or an impulse — it's a choice. There will be days in the future when we're hurt by a fellow human, and eventually we will either *choose* to forgive them, choosing to forgive those who have failed us or hurt us...

...or we won't.

There is no in-between. We cannot say one thing and then turn around and do the other. We can't proclaim God's forgiveness of sins while we secretly nurse our own grudges. We must choose. To forgive, just as *we have been forgiven*.

Let us hold unswervingly to the hope we profess,
for he who promised is faithful.
- Hebrews 10:23

Wild Faith

HAVE YOU EVER BEEN FACE DOWN IN THE DIRT OF LIFE? SHAKEN and confused, unsure of exactly how you ended up there? (*Prepare yourself... there's a rodeo analogy in your immediate future.*)

Eight seconds might sound like a short amount of time, but when you're on the back of a bucking Bronco holding on for dear life, it feels like a lifetime. If you don't have a tight grip on the reins, you're not just going to slip off gracefully, step back onto the ground and casually walk over to the safety of the stall. No sir. A loose grip will launch you into the air so far and so fast that when you come back down you won't know what hit you. (That is, unless the angry animal doesn't charge at a nearby clown, in which case you'll probably know *exactly* what hit you...)

The truth is simple: riding in a rodeo is not for wimps or those with a loose grip. Neither is holding onto your faith.

When life is racing around like a crazed creature from the pits and you're strapped on its back, you've got to hold your reins of faith tightly. Life will give you every good reason to loosen your grip, let go or even quit, telling you that your future holds nothing but failure and misery in store.

Don't believe it. Don't quit.

Reaffirm your grip and hang in there!

Set your face like flint and **Choose to Believe** in a future that will not only make sense when you step into it, but will also be *good*, *pleasing* and ***perfect***. Even if you can't see it from your perspective today, you can know it's what He has promised for your tomorrow.

Faith.

Grab hold of it with both hands and hold on.

Jesus would often slip away
to the wilderness and pray.
- Luke 5:16

Slipping Away

JUST LIKE YOU AND US, JESUS ALSO NEEDED A BREAK FROM THE constant demands of a busy life. He took time to recharge and spend dedicated, isolated time with his heavenly Father.

Even though he was God incarnate, Jesus didn't tap into his divine superpowers as the Son of God when it came to meeting life's challenges. Instead, when he was burdened or exhausted or needed to be refreshed, he would get away and pray. He would plug into the power and peace that could only be found in God's presence.

We would be wise to model the pace of our lives after him. Our culture has glorified those who work non-stop, the ones who charge forward and seize the day... and the night... and any other available second in order to get ahead. But it never ends. If we don't know where we're going or what the ultimate purpose is, we're just killing time on the treadmill of life.

Do you want more peace in your life? More direction? More wisdom and comfort and joy? Honest-to-God, sincere and lasting *joy*? Then make a date. Just you and Him. It doesn't have to be for hours, of course, but whatever time you invest in Him *will be rewarded*. Not with what you think you want, but what you genuinely *need*.

"Go to your private room and, when you have shut your door,
pray to your Father who is in that secret place."
- Matthew 6:6

Scheduled Silence

IF WE FIND OURSELVES REACHING A PLACE IN OUR LIVES WHERE we're in need of specific direction from God, we're going to have to take specific action first. We may need to make an extra effort to actually do something different if we want to get different results. Hearing from God typically requires dedicated focus on two key components: **time** and **silence**.

If we're craving His word, His wisdom and His comfort, we need to schedule time to pursue it. It's not enough to simply *want* it, no matter how sincerely or earnestly we may feel. We have to be willing to back up our emotions and intentions with *action*. We need to schedule — *actually schedule* — more silence and quiet opportunities into our lives. More time — minutes or hours — to sit and worship Him, to praise and to pray.

Our time will be better invested if we try to reduce the constant onslaught of our problems, our desires, our goals and our agendas, and instead choose to schedule and embrace the silence where He can be found.

Maybe this week is a good time to try to set aside a small slice of time to just... *listen.*

Also you shall purposely pull out for her some grain
from the bundles and leave it that she may glean,
and do not rebuke her. - Ruth 2:16

Handfuls On Purpose

EVERYTHING THAT WE RECEIVE IN THIS LIFE COMES FROM GOD.
Funny thing, though, it doesn't just magically manifest in our hands
or bank accounts. Instead, He uses other people to get it to us. It
comes *through* them, but we should never forget that the Lord is
ultimately the one who provides us with it all — our innate skills, our
job opportunities and promotions, and His extreme favor (even when
we don't deserve it or expect it).

This was the case with Ruth. Boaz wasn't just being generous
and compassionate for her, but he was especially interested in her.
She had won his heart with her humility and faithfulness to her
mother-in-law, as well as her love for God. God blessed her directly
— *through Boaz* — giving her more than enough.

May we all recognize the unique opportunities for generosity
when He presents them to us, and then respond with the same giving
heart that Boaz had toward Ruth.

Before I formed you in the womb I knew you,
before you were born I set you apart.
- Jeremiah 1:5

Purposed

Before the very beginning of the world, God knew you. He was thinking of *you*, anticipating *you* and who *you* would become — even before the foundation of the earth.

He was planning your life, eagerly looking forward to how it would unfold, day by day and year by year. Before you were ever created, God, the King of the Universe, was *excited* that you would one day be arriving on the scene. He thought of you and smiled!

Before you were formed as an embryo, knit together in the depths of your mother's womb, He knew you, watched you and was speaking forth His love for you. Before a single cell came to be, He was composing His plans and purposes for your life, long before you ever even took a single breath. Before your mother even knew she was carrying you, *God spoke life and love into your being.*

God had a vision for you and a divine destiny before you even existed. Before your parents or their parents or *their* parents before them, dating all the way back to eternity. Before anything came into being, the God of Heaven and Earth anticipated your arrival in this life.

Your life is not an accident.

You were created on purpose, *for* a purpose.

If you're discouraged or disillusioned or simply struggling with the idea that you have value and purpose and meaning, take a moment to stop and tell Him about it. Tell Him exactly how you feel, and ask Him to open your eyes and heart to see and receive the Truth about your life.

They will have no fear of bad news;
their hearts are steadfast, trusting in the LORD.
- Psalms 112:7

Mistake Weights

HAVE YOU EVER MET SOMEONE WHO WAS DOWNRIGHT TERRIFIED of making a mistake? Someone so riddled with self-doubt and fear that they're practically paralyzed because they're so incredibly scared of taking a misstep in their lives.

We don't have to be so afraid of screwing things up. If our hearts are pure and we're actively pursuing the Lord, we can cling to Him — even in our mistakes. Yes, we're human and yes, we will *all* make mistakes (large *and* small). It's inevitable. But we don't have to dread them, because God is in charge of these setbacks as well.

He's not going to allow disaster to swallow us whole simply because of our limited insight or inability to "do it right" all the time. We can trust that even in our mistakes, He will continue to orchestrate them for our good. We don't have to let the possibility of a mistake shackle us and weigh us down. Just keep pursuing Him.

He is faithful. He loves us.

Yet the Lord will not spare us from ever making mistakes because He knows it is through them that we must learn. He will allow us to make mistakes, knowing ahead of time that some lessons we can learn no other way. This is a generous and sincere act of love, even if we don't feel very loved at the time.

We don't have to be afraid of making mistakes in life. They are not only inevitable, they are for our benefit in the end, as we learn from them and move forward in life.

Everyone who confesses the name of the Lord
must turn away from wickedness.
- 2 Timothy 2:19

Turning Away

THERE ARE A LOT OF PEOPLE IN THE WORLD WHO LOVE THE *IDEA* of being a Christian without actually changing their lifestyle. They subscribe to the notion that there's a God, that we're all created beings, and they love the camaraderie and fellowship with other like-minded people. It's like belonging to a holy-roller country club.

Yet when it comes to admitting their sin and surrendering to His instruction and the Spirit's leading, committing their lives to obediently follow Jesus — they want nothing to do with Him. Sure, they'll still identify themselves as "Christian," talk about loving and following God, yet will be utterly unfamiliar with His Word, ignoring behaviors or actions He's clearly identified as sinful.

We don't get to choose what God classifies as sin and what He doesn't. *He* is the one who decides, *He* is the one who establishes what constitutes goodness and holiness and righteousness. We don't get to define them based on the shifting sands of our culture or how we "sincerely" we may feel about it.

We must all make a choice in life.

Turn away from ourselves and serve Him.

Or turn away from Him... and serve ourselves.

It can't be both.

But the time is coming, and has come,
when you will be scattered, each to his own home.
You will leave me all alone. Yet I am not alone, for my father is
with me. I have told you these things, so that in me
you may have peace. In this world you will have trouble.
But take heart! I have overcome the world.
- John 16:31-33

Scattered and Tattered and Peaceful

HERE JESUS WAS SPEAKING TO HIS DISCIPLES, ONCE MORE foretelling what was about to happen. And not surprisingly, it unfolded *exactly* as he predicted.

He was arrested.

They scattered.

And he was left utterly alone...

Yet even in his suffering, **God was with him**.

His words paint a similar picture for us today, foretelling a time when we as Christians will be equally divided and scattered. There *will* come a time in our lives when we will have trouble in this world. It's inevitable.

It's easy to focus on the first part, the trouble and promise of pain, but we don't have to hover on that bleak note. If we focus on that part and *only* that part, we're conveniently forgetting the rest of the story.

Yes, Jesus emphasizes that there are going to be dark times ahead of us, but then He encourages us. He tells us these things not to scare us, but specifically so we might have His *peace!* Because even when our world spirals violently out of control, we can rest knowing He has *overcome* the world. (Both our personal ones *and* that beautiful blue marble floating in space...)

Peace is possible — even when we're scratched and scattered, torn and tattered.

He Is With Us. Always.

My flesh and my heart may fail, but God
is the strength of my heart and my portion forever.
- Psalm 73:26

A Letter to the Hopeless One

YOU'RE CONFUSED, BEATEN DOWN AND FEELING INCREDIBLY, hopelessly depressed. You've been waiting for so long, and you can't help but wonder if anything is ever, *ever* going to change. What you've been desperately hoping would happen... hasn't. And even now, as the days and weeks and months have slipped by, you can feel the strength of your faith fading in the waiting.

Don't give up.

It's so easy to look at yesterday, point the finger and insist that God hasn't moved in the way you expected Him to. While this might be 100% true, just because you can't see Him working doesn't mean He's not there. Even His decision to delay something today doesn't prevent Him from acting tomorrow. Remind yourself that His timing is absolutely precise and without fault, even if *feels* late.

The truth of your yesterday doesn't have to define your truth today, or your reality tomorrow. **You can choose to trust Him, even when your heart is aching.** Cry out for comfort. Pray for perspective. Request relief. But afterwards, even if those things aren't provided to you in abundance or within the time frame you want?

Choose to trust Him anyway.

Watch out! Be on your guard against all kinds of greed;
life does not consist in an abundance of possessions.
- Luke 12:14

Do Not Feed the Bear

GREED IS UGLY. *BUTT UGLY.*

Why? Because even though it may begin on the inside of us, it soon reveals itself on the outside. Unlike so many other sins that might plague us, we can't hide greed. No, Greed manifests quite quickly, and everyone around us will see it rear its ugly head in due time if they hang out with us long enough.

Greed is hungry. *Ravenously hungry.*

Greed's hunger is insatiable, and no matter how much we might have today, how much we've been given up to this point, **Greed always wants More**. If we're not on guard, we'll mistakenly assume that more is the answer to life's problems.

More money. **More** recognition, *more* advancement, *MORE* responsibility, *MORE* (insert your personal lack in life here). Without a proper perspective, we'll start believing that **more** will make us infinitely happier.

Wanna know a secret? It won't.

Why not? Because **Greed is an ugly, hungry black bear** with a bottomless pit in its core. And no matter what we fill it with, regardless of what we throw at it or attempt to feed it with... it will always, *always* want more. That is its nature.

Resist the temptation to feed that creepy critter.

Stop feeding the bear.

He who digs a hole and scoops it out falls into the pit he has made.
The trouble he causes recoils on himself;
his violence comes down on his own head. - Psalm 7:15-16

The wicked are ensnared by the work of their hands.
- Psalms 9:16

Ensnared

TIME AND TIME AGAIN SCRIPTURE TELLS US THE BENEFITS OF living a righteous life and choosing God, as well as the folly of choosing evil and causing trouble for others.

Maybe you're at a place in your life right now where you feel attacked or discouraged because of something someone else has done (or worse, is currently doing today). Maybe they're just misguided, or maybe they actually *are* bent on evil and making trouble. Regardless, one thing is sure: if they're truly working with evil intent, wanting to attack for no good reason, it will backfire.

The holes they're digging? They're going to fall face-first into them themselves. The trouble they're stirring up? It will rebound against them, and by their own hands they will be ensnared. If they are spreading lies, the truth will eventually come out and they will inevitably be caught in their own web.

If you believe in the Bible and the truth that it contains, you really don't have to worry about people doing you wrong in this world. God is just. So don't try to fix everything yourself. Instead, maybe now is the time to take a step back and permit Him be the one who will justify you and lift you up in the end.

Trust in the Lord with all your heart
and do not lean on your own understanding.
- Proverbs 3:5

Trust Issues

"DO *NOT* LEAN ON YOUR OWN UNDERSTANDING."

Without a doubt, this is one of the most difficult commands we will ever face in our lives as Christians. We're far more likely to assess our circumstances and make swift, snap judgments about how best to handle them. It's what we've done all of our lives, from childhood to adulthood! Study a situation, reach a few educated conclusions, make decisions and then take decisive action. Problem solved!

Certainly, leaning on our own understanding can work wonders at times (especially for our fragile egos...). But sometimes our lack of insight can leave us feeling discouraged or even afraid for the future. From that perspective, our problems sometimes appear so overwhelming or impossible that we simply can't see a good solution.

As much as we want to rely on it, our perspective is actually severely limited. Why? Because it's always focused squarely on one single point of weakness: ourselves.

Thankfully, God doesn't look at our problems the same way. He can see the end from the beginning, and is happy to lead us along the path from one to the other. It's not always going to be a pleasant stroll, of course, but we can continue to trust the One who made the map to be our Guide.

With God all things are possible. - Matthew 19:26

Standing On the Impossible

THESE DAYS IT'S EASY TO GET WORRIED AND DISCONTENT ABOUT the direction this world is going. So often we're like Peter, walking on the water of our faith. We're doing just fine until we see the size and intensity of the waves around us, hungrily lapping at our ankles, our shins, our knees and on up as we slowly start to sink.

We begin to worry about what's going to happen to us... or what's *not* going to happen, as the case may be. We start worrying about what's already happened... or what *hasn't* happened yet. The waves of fear and doubt come hard and fast, from every direction, and before we know it we've taken our eyes off of Jesus and started thinking how in the world we can save ourselves from sinking.

Self-preservation. It's a strong instinct.

Yet if we'll just stay focused on Jesus... focused on seeking His face, ignoring the distractions and gravity of the world around us... we *will* rise above it. We will stand with our Savior, upright and balanced in impossible places we never could have imagined we'd be.

Don't lose hope. *Don't lose sight of Him.*

Grab His hand. Look up, and be determined to stand in the safest place you can ever be — right by your Savior's side.

Naked I came from my mother's womb,
and naked I will depart. The Lord gave and the Lord
has taken away; may the name of the Lord be praised.
- Job: 1:21

The Finish Line

THE ONE WHO DIES WITH THE MOST TOYS WINS.

This was a popular bumper sticker quote many years ago, and it aptly summarizes the philosophy many of us still live by. Without opportunities for growth or spiritual maturity, we're not much different as adults than we were as toddlers. We still think our happiness hinges on surrounding ourselves with every trinket or toy in sight. Every pretty doll, fast car, new playhouse or shiny gadget... we eagerly scoop them up, making a mountain of Stuff where we can sit and feel satisfied.

But sooner or later we'll come to realize that it's just not enough. The things we had yesterday won't give us the same emotional high tomorrow, and we'll soon be embarking on the desperate search for more to fill the need. More dolls, more vehicles, more gadgets, more levels of success... more, more *more*.

We forget what Job figured out so long ago: we can't take it with us. *None of it.* All these things we're doing with our lives, the Stuff we're spending our money and time on? Unless they have eternal worth, we're simply surrounding ourselves with Stuff to make us feel better or more important. We came into this world with absolutely nothing, and aside from our relationship with Jesus and those around us, we will take nothing with us into the next life.

People matter the most. Stuff is... just stuff.

(And we can't take any of it with us.)

Is God moving you to invest your time or resources in a different way this week? Maybe somewhere new? Or in some*one*?

And without faith it is impossible to please God.
- Hebrews 11:6

No Faith? Impossible!

THE BIBLE IS CLEAR: WITHOUT FAITH IT IS ABSOLUTELY, utterly impossible to please God. But why, exactly, is faith so incredibly important? Because faith highlights where we tend to put our trust in life.

God wants us to trust Him completely, honestly and intimately. He doesn't want to be an afterthought, He wants to be the *forethought*. He wants you to know Him and love Him so clearly that the idea of *not* trusting Him would be absolutely ludicrous.

If you're reading this today and your feelings are perfectly lined up with your faith? Fantastic. More power to you. But as we all know from experience, feelings by themselves aren't always dependable, and there's going to come a day when the feelings inside that soft, human heart of yours will tell you that trusting in God isn't going to work anymore. You'll be tempted to jump in and try to make things happen in *your* time, with *your* power.

Any guesses how that's going to end?

Having faith is important. Just make sure you've placed it in the One who is actually *faithful*.

Give thanks in all circumstances. — *1 Thessalonians 5:18*

The Negative Zone

NEGATIVITY IS KIND OF LIKE A VAMPIRE, IN MANY WAYS. IT attaches itself to you somewhat unexpectedly, leeching the energy and life right out of you. Before you know it, you're all sickly and pale and coughing up dust.

Okay, maybe that's a little overdramatic, but the point is this: negativity can be a powerful force, and if you don't actively resist it, it will attempt to consume you.

I once worked with a woman who was one of the most negative people I had ever met. She had a perpetual frown on her face, and everything she said — I'm not kidding, *EVERYTHING* — was tinged with a note of defeat, depression and pure, uncut negativity. She was Debbie Downer incarnate, and I could only stand to be around her for a minute or two before I conjured up a reason to be elsewhere. *ANY*where else. It was borderline unbearable.

Don't be like Debbie Downer.

Refuse to let your thoughts derail your life (and the lives of those around you). **FIGHT IT.** No matter how bad you think your situation is, God can show you what's right about it, what's *good* about it, if you'll only take the time to ask Him. And when you find yourself getting sprayed by the torrential downpour of someone else's rainy day parade? Try to have patience, see them as God sees them and don't let yourself be sucked into the sphere of their negativity.

Giants

DAVID AND GOLIATH. IT'S A FAMILIAR STORY WE'VE HEARD since childhood. It's a story we relate to as we each fight our unique, personal battles — our Goliaths. In Samuel 17, David shows us a side of God that we can gain much strength and reliance from. Listen to the words he uses when he confronts Goliath in verses 45-46.

> *"You come to me with sword, spear, and javelin, but I come to you in the name of the Lord of Heaven's Armies - the God of the armies of Israel, whom you have defied. Today, the Lord will conquer you, and I will kill you and cut off your head."*

We often find ourselves attacking our problems with man-made solutions. Swords, Spears, Javelins — all of these are weapons that we fashion with our own hands. Sometimes we put too much confidence in ourselves. Our plans, our money and income, the personal measure of our power, position and influence.

David came to the battle with a *name*. That's it.

He stood there on the battlefield in front of Goliath and the armies with nothing but a name.

Makes you think, doesn't it? In our own lives, how much do we really trust that name? The name of the Lord of Heaven's armies. Do we stand and represent Him? Do we realize that *the Lord* is the one who does the conquering, rather than us?

David's comment reveals a lot about *who* does *what*. It is **the Lord who conquers**. David killed Goliath and cut off his head — yes, he did the physical work and it was hard work. But it was *the Lord* who conquered.

Father, remind us of this truth when we stand in your name. We overcome our giants only because You conquer them for us. Help us keep you at the front of our battle lines, fighting in Your power rather than our manmade strength.

Blessed is the man whom God corrects;
do not despise the discipline of the Almighty.
For he wounds, but he also binds up;
he injures, but his hands also heal.
- Job 5:17-18

Blessed Discipline

DISCIPLINE IS OFTEN CONFUSED WITH PUNISHMENT.

It doesn't have to be negative, however. Discipline, by its purest definition, means "disciple-making." Raising up, shaping and molding someone else for their good.

God is always loving, and absolutely everything He does is good. He is always on our side, and He always wants what is best for us — every single day. So when He disciplines us, we don't have to wonder about His true motives or worry that He suddenly resents us. He doesn't.

God disciplines those He loves, and the man that He corrects is *blessed* because of it.

Patient endurance is what you need now,
so that you will continue to do God's will.
Then you will receive all that he has promised.
- Hebrews 10:36

Patient Endurance

THERE'S A FINE LINE BETWEEN WORKS AND FAITH, ISN'T THERE? We're saved by faith and not by works, that any man should be able to boast about what he's done. Yet we're still called to be faithful in doing God's work, faithful in doing what He has prepared for us.

Doing what He wants us to do requires **Patient Endurance.** Confident trust in God allows us to wake up each day and press on. We're not always going to understand *why* God did something or asked us to make certain sacrifices. Faith requires that we continue to cling to what He has promised — whether or not we can see those promises taking shape in the distance.

One element which stands out in this particular verse is that we will *receive* what He has promised. It doesn't say that we will *earn* what He has promised. This is the tricky part — the "fine line," if you will. We work with patient endurance, knowing that we will receive what He has promised, and expecting with faith all that He has promised, but also knowing that we are not *earning* His blessing.

Because we are *already* blessed.

We don't have to scramble about, trying to earn the blessing we already possess. Realize His love is greater than us and all of our attempts at good works. He loves us — He loves *you* — today.

Many, Lord my God, are the wonders you have done,
the things you planned for us. None can compare with you;
were I to speak and tell of your deeds,
they would be too many to declare. - Psalm 40:5

Eternal Focus

GOD HAS DONE SO MANY WONDERFUL, AMAZING THINGS, NOT only in the general world, but in our lives specifically. If we stop long enough to be honest with ourselves, we can look back on our history and see — even during the painful times — He was there. His faithfulness may not have revealed itself in the method or timing we expected, hoped or prayed for, but with hindsight it will usually shine through with striking brilliance and clarity.

When we are caught up in the moment, drowning in the pain or confusion, it's easy for us to lose focus. We need to take our eyes off of what we see today, right in front of us, and take on His *eternal* perspective. He has wonderful things planned for us tomorrow and beyond, *regardless* of what we're seeing and experiencing today.

What about you? How do you feel God might be challenging you to change your focus this week? Maybe He wants you to look at a current situation with new eyes, or a new understanding?

Lord God, answer me, answer me,
that the people may know that you are God.
- 1 Kings 18:37

Make Yourself Known

THIS WAS THE RISKY, IMPASSIONED PRAYER OF ELIJAH AS HE confronted the prophets of Baal. Can you imagine praying this prayer? Standing in front of all those people, many of them angry and ready to kill you? Risking everything? (Well, mainly your reputation and God's...)

So what about you? What is the issue that you're facing today in your life where you are earnestly *pleading* with God to work in? To make Himself *known*? To show His power and faithfulness? Are you willing to accept that He might just wait a while longer before He finally reveals Himself?

It's tempting to interpret God's delay or perceived lack of action as His indifference or unwillingness to answer. Yet if we will cling to what we know, to the truth of Who He Is, we might just see miracles that we could never imagine happening in our lifetimes.

*Be very careful, then, how you live —
not as unwise but as wise, making the most
of every opportunity, because the days are evil.*
- Ephesians 5:15-16

Time to Give

CONTRARY TO POPULAR BELIEF, THERE IS SOMETHING WE ALL have the ability to give that is far more costly, valuable and in limited quantity than money itself.

And what is this ever-present, fleeting resource, you ask?

Time. *Your* time, to be specific.

How is time more valuable than moneyk? Well, it's really quite simple: money can be *earned*. We can always do something to create more money or generate more income in our lives. Create something, sell something, trade something, provide something... we can always come up with creative and innovative ways to make more money.

Time, on the other hand, is an extremely limited commodity. It is given to us every day, but we cannot make it ourselves. As much as we would like to, there's simply no way we can generate more time than what we already have.

Of course, there are many places we can choose to spend our time. Entertainment. Work. Escape. We've discovered, however, that relationships are the best places to invest our time. Children, friends, family... whatever relationships we've been blessed with, they *all* need a healthy investment of our time to thrive. Without a constant influx of time, these relationships slowly shrivel up and die.

You've been given a virtual fortune.

Share your wealth. Share your *self*.

Tomorrow isn't a given.

Consider investing your time in someone else today.

Set a guard over my mouth, O Lord;
keep watch over the door of my lips.
- Psalm 141:3

Mute Me

IF I WAS EVER GOING TO GET A SCRIPTURE VERSE TATTOOED ON
my body somewhere, this would probably be the one. Why? Because
this is a prayer that I find myself praying repeatedly and on a constant
basis. (Especially as I get older and "wiser" in my own eyes.)

When I was growing up I wanted to be a Christian comedian. I
enjoyed making people laugh, to use humor to alleviate tension in a
conversation while also communicating God's love. I'm not a
professional, but I still love doing this. Yet if there's one thing we
need to remember about humor, it's that it is exceptionally subjective.

What one person finds hilarious, the next will think is outright
stupid. Or even hurtful. There have been many, many times that my
sarcastic wit was unintentionally been responsible for bruising a
heart rather than blessing it. James was right when he expressed the
dangers of the tongue and the difficulty in keeping it tamed.

So I'm constantly praying that God would set some kind of a
virtual guard over my mouth, an invisible muzzle or filter of sorts, and
help me keep watch over the words that I say. I envision a mute
button in place, so that maybe the Holy Spirit would just cut my
volume off before I actually *say* something I'll regret.

How about you? Do you find it difficult to keep your lips zipped
sometimes? How do you think God can help?

But to you who are listening I say: Love your enemies,
do good to those who hate you, bless those who curse you,
pray for those who mistreat you.
- Luke 6:27-28

Love Them

THESE WORDS OF JESUS ARE CONTRARY TO EVERYTHING WE FEEL as human beings. After all, our enemies are... well... *enemies*. Every emotion churning inside of us, every natural inclination of our heart is to *defeat* them. To try to *eliminate* them. To embarrass, pay back and do anything else we can think of just to get *rid* of them.

And yet, here Jesus is telling us to love them. To *bless* them, actually. To somehow treat our enemies *completely opposite* of how we naturally want to treat them. Impossible, right? Completely unrealistic. So why does He say we should do this?

It's because He understood the powerful, poisonous nature of unforgiveness and hatred. He knew that we only damage ourselves when we fill our hearts with these things that will weigh us down rather than give us the freedom they promise.

Your anger is real. Your pain and your bitterness and the justification are all real, and you feel them intensely (possibly daily). But it is far more important for us to remain obedient to Christ's words, to stay pure-hearted with a clear conscience rather than exact vengeance on our many enemies.

If this is you and you're struggling with resentment and bitterness today, why not give it up? Open your hands and your heart, confess it to God and let the healing begin.

One person gives freely, yet gains even more;
another withholds unduly, but comes to poverty.
A generous person will prosper;
whoever refreshes others will be refreshed.
- Proverbs 11:24-25

Trust For Tomorrow

GOD DOESN'T WANT US TO LIVE OUR LIVES SHACKLED WITH A scarcity mentality, always feeling like we never have "enough." He wants us to live in abundance, with *freedom*.

Freedom to love, freedom to live and freedom to give.

So many times we see ourselves as lacking. We have a nagging fear that if we give something today, we won't have enough tomorrow. We're taught again and again to save, to squirrel away our scraps for tomorrow. To a degree, this makes perfect sense. We *should* be wise with our finances and resources and prepare for the future.

Yet there's another part of this philosophy that's rarely addressed. You see, if we're trying to scramble and fill our barns and buckets and pockets out of fear for the ever-present threat of "Tomorrow," what is our underlying belief? Do we not believe that God is good, powerful, and more than able to provide for us in the future? Or is it all up to our own human effort, our limited wisdom and sheer grit to make tomorrow a more bearable, comfortable living?

We need a balance. The Bible makes it clear: a generous person *will* prosper, and whoever refreshes others *will* be refreshed. There's a direct link between our *giving today* and *having enough tomorrow*.

God rewards generosity, and not just financially. We can give our time, our talents, our resources — whatever He's placed in our hands. But first we must be willing to open our bunched up fists of fear, the terror of not having enough tomorrow, and **Let Go**.

Are there ways you feel God wants you to give today? And if so, will you trust Him to continue to provide for you tomorrow?

Moreover, demons came out of many people,
shouting, "You are the Son of God!" But he rebuked them
and would not allow them to speak,
because they knew he was the Messiah.
- Luke 4:41

Hard Facts vs. Honest Faith

BELIEVING IN JESUS FOR OUR ULTIMATE SALVATION INVOLVES more than just intellectual assessment and acceptance. The Bible makes it clear: even the demons believed in the truth that Jesus was the Son of God.

Clearly, "belief" isn't enough to save us.

Unfortunately, it is this exact type of "faith" that we see common around the world today. People love the *idea* of Jesus, and the majority of them will readily profess that he was "a good man," or a "good teacher" who set a good example for us to live up to. Sadly, that's where it ends, with Jesus being defined as "good" but not God.

We need more. We need to cross over from simply believing the facts of Jesus' historical existence to accepting — in faith — His divine nature and His sacrifice. We need to reach out and actually accept His gift, instead of just acknowledging He gave it.

The steadfast love of the Lord never ceases;
his mercies never come to an end;
they are new every morning;
great is your faithfulness.
- Lamentations 3:22-23

Thank You For Today

LORD, WE JUST WANT TO THANK YOU FOR TODAY.

We want to thank you for everything You've given us up to now.

Lord, thank you for our health. While it may not be perfect, and there are many things we wish would be different, we are very grateful for what we have today. We can breathe, we can see, we're alive. Help us to rely on Your grace and Your providence today, to recognize those gifts that You've already given us.

Father, we want to thank you for Your patience. So many times we will condemn ourselves because we feel we're not where we want to be yet, spiritually and emotionally. So many times we feel like we're not good enough, that we don't measure up.

Thank you that You don't condemn us. You are not looking at us in constant disapproval. You love us, recognizing us as ongoing works in progress. So we thank You for that. Thank you for loving us through all the changes and transitions in our hearts, regardless of how slowly they may come about.

Thank you for the changes You've *already* made in our lives, and thank you for the changes that You've pre-orchestrated for our future. Please give us patience with ourselves, knowing that life takes time. Help us to be thankful for where we are *today*, instead of constantly looking back and longing for yesterday or trying to push forward and live in tomorrow. Please help us to stay focused on the gifts You've given us right now, *today*.

Who are Kevin & Kim Mills?

After we met on a blind date at **John Brown University** in **Siloam Springs, Arkansas**, we swiftly fell for each other. (Despite it being a carefully-designed blind date disaster...) We were married in 1993, and soon the adventure of a lifetime began!

Over the years, we've hopped around the globe numerous times, and now have many places we can call home: **Tulsa, Oklahoma; St. Louis, Missouri; Edmond, Oklahoma; Lubbock, Texas; Lexington, Kentucky; Washington, D.C.** and now for the second time in our lives, **Papua, Indonesia**. After holding a wide variety of professional positions (*market research, teaching, graphic design, law enforcement, etc.*) we felt the Lord calling us to return to the mission field back in **2013**.

So after much prayer and confirmations, The K Mills Family (along with our three K Clones — **Kyler, Kaleb** and **Kara**) abandoned our comfortable American lives and relocated to Papua, one of the most remote and isolated places on earth. Serving through **Mission Aviation Fellowship** (www.maf.org), we started working at **Hillcrest School** (www.hismk.org) as Dorm Parents. Over the next four years we created a fun-loving, faith-filled home to over 30 missionary kids as their parents served elsewhere in the country doing Bible translation and teaching, community development, evangelism and more.

In 2017, we transitioned to the academic side of Hillcrest, teaching various classes (*Math, Yearbook, Senior Seminar, Creative Writing*) and later working in **Administration** and **Communications**, where we continue to serve today. If you'd like to know more about our ministry or want to become more directly involved in supporting our mission, please visit www.maf.org/mills or call **Mission Aviation Fellowship** at **1-800-359-7623**.

Thank you for your constant love & support!

Kevin & Kim

HOSTEL 1
2013-2017

For over 75 years, **Mission Aviation Fellowship** has used aviation to share the love of Jesus Christ with isolated people who have not yet heard the Gospel.

MAF operates a fleet of 47 light aircraft from 14 bases in eight countries in *Africa, Asia, Eurasia* and *Latin America*. Their pilots save valuable travel time and cover seemingly impossible distances in minutes or hours, compared to days of traveling by foot, road or river. Each year they fly over two million nautical miles to speed the work of *more than 500 Christian and humanitarian organizations.*

MAF flights support indigenous churches and local evangelists, create access to medical care, provide disaster relief and help make the impossible community development projects possible. **They are constantly working to see isolated people changed by the love of Christ** in some of the most remote places on earth.

Mission Aviation Fellowship
P.O. Box 47, Nampa, ID 83653
(800) FLYS-MAF (359-7623)
www.maf.org

MAF is a 501(c)3 not-for-profit charity and a member
of ECFA (*Evangelical Council for Financial
Accountability*) and Accord Network.